The Bard in Brief

Robert W. Wolfe

The Bard in Brief
Short Quotations from the Plays of William Shakespeare

Edited by Robert W. Wolfe

VANTAGE PRESS
New York

FIRST EDITION

All rights reserved, including the right of
reproduction in whole or in part in any form.

Copyright © 1996 by Robert W. Wolfe

Published by Vantage Press, Inc.
516 West 34th Street, New York, New York 10001

Manufactured in the United States of America
ISBN: 0-533-11885-9

Library of Congress Catalog Card No.: 96-90079

0 9 8 7 6 5 4 3 2 1

To my three daughters, to whom I have always tried to avoid being a Lear in anger, for they rarely gave me cause; and from whom I have received joy in great measure, for which I am evermore grateful.

Table Of Contents

Preface ix

Acknowledgements xiii

List of Subjects xv

Quotations, Arranged by Subject 1

Glossary 281

Shakespeare, Genius or Fraud? 307

Index of Plays 311

Preface

We all know that Shakespeare is a great author, but most of us find that it is not easy to sit down and read Shakespeare's plays. It is much more interesting to see his plays than read them because the action and the actors make the meaning of the words more understandable. Even so, the casual listener can easily miss much of the subtle meaning of the lines. Since I found that I greatly enjoyed hearing the poetry of the lines when seeing a play, I determined to study Shakespeare's plays to improve my understanding and thereby enhance my enjoyment.

This study was a labor of many years, of course, and as I read the plays I would do so with pen in hand and mark a few lines that especially struck me. "There's a gem" I would say to myself, and perhaps read it aloud to hear how it sounded to the ear.

To share my favorite "gems" with others, I have collected these short Shakespearean quotations in this book. I hope you will find browsing through the book an easy way to enjoy Shakespeare's words without having to become "seriously involved."

To enhance the usefulness of this collection, I have organized the quotations according to subject. Thus, if you are writing a letter, and wish to add some Shakespearean flair to a point you are making, this will make it easier to find the appropriate quotation. Or, if you are going to see a particular play, you can review the quotations in the book from that play and anticipate the lines. This may add a little "zing" to the performance. To facilitate finding the quotations, I also have created an index of the quotations by play.

For those who have a nodding interest in Shakespeare, but might find the meaning of some of the quotations somewhat obscure, I also have provided an interpretation in modern English for each quotation. Finally, I have provided the speaker and the listener, the name of the play, the scene number, and the line number for each quotation. The line numbers correspond to those in *William Shakespeare: The Complete Works*, The Viking Press, New York, 1969.

There are many words and phrases that are either obscure or used by Shakespeare with a meaning that is different from that to which we are accustomed. (For example, the word *still* is most often used by Shakespeare to mean always, rather than motionless.) For those readers who wish to determine the meaning of these words or phrases, a glossary is provided in the back of the book. Because it may not be clear to the reader at which word some phrases might begin, I have arranged the glossary by page number rather than alphabetically. Thus, if you are unsure about some word or phrase in a quotation, you should check in the glossary for the words/phrases listed for that page number, and it is likely that you will find the definition.

No words have been added, I assure you, but to enhance generality I have occasionally omitted names of characters in the play or the lines of an intermediate speaker when they detract from the general meaning of the quotation.

You will see that the first lines of some of the quotations are indented. This is because the first sentence of the quotation begins part of the way along a line that is written in the classic iambic pentameter, and I felt the missing portion of the line should be indicated by the indentation. Also, an occasional "and" or "for" or similar word with which the first line of a quotation begins has been omitted. This is because the word is a continuation of a previous line that has not been included, and the word would be awkward if it were left in place. Finally, you will find an occasional word with the notation èd. This means that the ed is spoken as a separate syllable to satisfy the iambic meter.

Of course, you need not wait to pick up the book until you are in search of a quotation or are about to attend a play. I hope you will find it interesting and entertaining to browse through it for the sheer pleasure of finding out what the "greatest English language author" had to say on a total of two hundred and seventy-nine subjects. Note that, because of their content, some quotations are listed under more than one subject.

My fond hope is that, even if you are only a casual reader, this book will spark your interest to explore the expansive world that Shakespeare created. It is a world populated with fascinating people from the wide spectrum of humanity who reveal themselves in lines that range from the sublime to the bawdy, from the amusing to the tragic, and from the clever to the profound. When spoken, their words "creep in our ears" with "the touches of sweet harmony," as the Bard would say.

                                            Robert W. Wolfe
                                            Pittsburgh, Pennsylvania
                                            1996

Acknowledgments

A man is blessed if he has friends and relatives who are interested in him and in the activities and projects he may engage in, and I am a man who finds himself so blessed. He is further fortunate if, in a particular project such as this book, he finds that he has friends and relatives who are not only interested, but also knowledgeable, and can provide valuable observations and opinions about various technical and aesthetic details of the project.

It is with much gratitude, therefore, that I acknowledge the help of my three daughters, Ruth Anne, Jennifer, and Elizabeth, my sisters Edith and Dorothy, and my former wife Dolores. I also thank my friend Nancy, who provided encouragement and demonstrated forbearance during the long gestation of this book.

The illustrations in the book (aside from the face of Shakespeare, which I sketched myself) were taken with permission from *Big Book of Graphic Designs and Devices* by Typony, Inc., Dover Publications, New York, 1990.

Most of the definitions in the glossary are based on annotations from *William Shakespeare: The Complete Works*, The Viking Press, New York, 1969, and *The Yale Shakespeare*, Yale University Press, New Haven, 1926. Some are from the *Oxford English Dictionary*, Oxford University Press, Oxford, 1971, and some are the interpretation of the editor.

◊ List of Subjects ◊

Acceptance 1	Compulsion 28	Disdain 71
Acting 2	Confidence 28	Disgrace 72
Action 2	Conflict 29	Dissemblance 72
Adversity 3	Confusion 29	Dissipation 72
Advice 4	Conscience 30	Distinction 73
Age 5	Consideration 31	Distrust 73
Allure 8	Consolation 32	Doubts 74
Ambition 8	Contrition 32	Drama 75
Anticipation 10	Coolness 33	Dreams 77
Apology 11	Courage 33	Drunkenness 77
Appearance 12	Courtship 36	Duty. 79
Appreciation 13	Cowardice 37	Education 80
Apprehension 14	Curses 37	Egocentricity 80
Attitude 15	Cycles 38	Enlightenment 81
Awareness 16	Danger 39	Entertainment 81
Baldness 16	Death 41	Ephemeral 82
Beauty 17	Deceit 53	Evil 82
Behavior 20	Deception 55	Excess 85
Blessing 21	Decline 61	Excitement 87
Bombast 21	Degradation 63	Expectation 88
Bore 22	Demagoguery 63	Failure 88
Caution 22	Demise 64	Faithfulness 89
Chance 24	Despair 64	Fate 91
Chaos 24	Desperation 66	Faults 96
Character 25	Despondency 66	Fear 97
Charity 25	Devil 67	Fishing 101
Cheerfulness 26	Devotion 67	Flattery 101
Choice 26	Dilemma 68	Folly 102
Cleverness 27	Directness 68	Foolishness 103
Comfort 27	Disappointment ... 69	Fools 105

List of Subjects (cont'd)

Forboding 105	Impertinence 134	Music 181
Forgiveness 106	Importance 134	Mystery 182
Fortune 106	Imprudence 135	Name 183
Frankness 107	Infidelity 136	Nature 183
Friendship 108	Ingratitude 136	New Beginnings 185
Generosity 111	Injustice 137	Nobility 185
Gentleness 111	Insanity 140	Obsession 187
Gold 112	Insecurity 140	Opinion 188
Good Fortune 112	Jealousy 141	Opportunity 188
Goodness 113	Joy 143	Optimism 189
Greatness 113	Judgment 144	Pain 190
Greed 115	Justice 146	Parting 190
Grief 116	Law 146	Passion 191
Guilt 120	Lethargy 147	Patience 191
Happiness 121	Life 147	Peace 192
Hate 121	Limitations 149	Penitence 193
Historic Event 123	Love 150	Perceptiveness ... 193
Holidays 123	Lust 167	Persistence 194
Honesty 124	Mankind 168	Pettiness 194
Honor 124	Marriage 168	Philosophy 195
Hope 126	Medicine 171	Pity 196
Hospitality 128	Melancholy 172	Plans 197
Humility 129	Men 172	Pleasure 197
Hypocrisy 129	Mercy 173	Politics 198
Idleness 130	Merriment 176	Possessions 198
Ignorance 131	Misery 176	Power 199
Illegitimacy 131	Mistake(s) 176	Praise 199
Illness 132	Misunderstndng. 178	Prayer 200
Imagination 132	Modesty 178	Prediction 200
Immoderation 133	Money 178	Preparation 201
Impatience 133	Moonlight 179	Prevention 202
Imperatives 134	Mortality 179	Prey 203

xvi

List of Subjects (cont'd)

Pride 203	Sarcasm 225	Thinking 251
Prodigality 204	Satisfaction 225	Time 251
Profit 204	Self-control 226	Tragedy 255
Promptness 205	Self-deception ... 226	Trap 255
Protest 205	Self-deprecation 227	Treason 255
Prudence 205	Self-examination 227	Truth 256
Public Opinion .. 207	Self-harm 227	Tyranny 257
Rage 207	Self-interest 229	Understanding ... 258
Rashness 208	Self-reliance 229	Unhappiness 259
Reasoning 209	Senses 231	Unkindness 260
Rebirth 210	Sex 231	Unsociable 261
Redundancy 210	Shyness 232	Valor 261
Reformation 211	Simpleness 233	Vengeance 263
Regret 212	Sin 234	Verbosity 263
Religion 213	Slander 236	Vice 265
Religious 213	Sleep 238	Villainy 265
Remoteness 214	Solace 240	Virginity 266
Repentance 214	Solitude 241	Virtue 266
Reproach 215	Sorrow 241	Vows 269
Reproof 215	Spectacle 244	Vulnerability 270
Reputation 215	Sport 244	War 271
Resourcefulness 219	Success 244	Warning 272
Responsibility 220	Succession 245	Weakness 272
Revelation 220	Suicide 246	Willfulness 272
Revenge 221	Sunrise 246	Wine 273
Righteousness 221	Superior 248	Wisdom 273
Ripeness 222	Tears 248	Wives 276
Rudeness 222	Temptation 248	Women 277
Rumor 223	Terror. 250	Worry 278
Sadness 224	Theater 250	Writing 279
Salesmanship 225	Theft 251	Youth 279

◊ Quotations by Subject ◊

Acceptance

**Things without all remedy
Should be without regard. What's done is done.**
        Lady Macbeth to Macbeth
        MACBETH
        Act III, Scene ii, Line 11

Situations that cannot be corrected should be ignored. What has been done is over with.

**What's gone and what's past help
Should be past grief.**
        Paulina to Lord
        WINTER'S TALE
        Act III, Scene ii, Line 220

What has previously happened and cannot be corrected should be no longer grieved over.

Acting

The purpose of playing, both at the first and now, was and is, to hold, as 'twere, the mirror up to nature, to show virtue her own feature, scorn her own image, and the very age and body of the time his form and pressure

Hamlet to the Players
HAMLET
Act III, Scene ii, Line 19

The purpose of plays and acting is and always has been to comment on the human condition, and to provide an image on the stage of the many emotions and conditions of the human drama.

Action

**Talkers are no good doers. Be assured:
We go to use our hands, and not our tongues.**

Murderer to Richard
RICHARD III
Act I, Scene iii, Line 350

People who talk a lot are not effective at taking action.
Do not worry, we plan to act, not to talk.

Action (cont'd)

Strong reasons makes strange actions.
Lewis to Pandulph
KING JOHN
Act III, Scene iv, Line 182

Important reasons justify unusual actions.

Be great in act, as you have been in thought.
Bastard to John
KING JOHN
Act V, Scene i, Line 4

Act boldly to carry out your plans or promote your viewpoint.

If it were done when 'tis done, then 'twere well It were done quickly.
Macbeth, aside
MACBETH
Act I, Scene vii, Line 1

If a difficult deed is to be done, it is better to do it without delay.

Adversity

Sweet are the uses of adversity.
Duke Senior to all
AS YOU LIKE IT
Act II, Scene i, Line 12

Adversity can result in many benefits to a person.

Advice

**Give every man thine ear, but few thy voice;
Take each man's censure, but reserve thy judgment.**

Polonius to Laertes
HAMLET
Act I, Scene iii, Line 68

Listen to everyone, but speak in confidence to very few. Consider each man's judgment, but do not voice your own too casually.

**Kill thy physician, and the fee bestow
Upon the foul disease.**

Kent to Lear
King Lear
Act I, Scene I, Line 163

If you don't listen to good advice, you will be aiding the very thing that's causing you harm.

**You cram these words into mine ears against
The stomach of my sense.**

Alonso to Gonzalo
THE TEMPEST
Act II, Scene I, Line 102

You force your words on me against my wishes.

Age

**O, grief hath changed me since you saw me last,
And careful hours, with Time's deformèd hand,
Have written strange defeatures in my face.**

Egeon to Antipholus E.
COMEDY OF ERRORS
Act V, Scene i, Line 298

Living with grief over a long time period has aged my appearance.

A man loves the meat in his youth that he cannot endure in his age.

Benedict in soliloquy
MUCH ADO ABOUT NOTHING
Act II, Scene iii, Line 218

As a man ages, his attitude toward some things changes.

**Last scene of all,
That ends this strange eventful history,
Is second childishness and mere oblivion,
Sans teeth, sans eyes, sans taste, sans everything.**

Jacques to all
AS YOU LIKE IT
Act II, Scene vii, Line 163

The last stage of life, which brings to an end the unusual and eventful life story, is a return to child-like behavior and a lack of awareness, without teeth, eyes, or taste, and then the loss of all sensations of worthwhile life.

Age (cont'd)

If to be old and merry be a sin, then many an old host that I know is damned.
Falstaff to Prince Hal
1 HENRY IV
Act II, Scene iv, Line 448

If it is a sin to be old and full of fun, then many an old man that I know is going to hell.

Care keeps his watch in every old man's eye, And where care lodges sleep will never lie.
Friar to Romeo
ROMEO AND JULIET
Act II, Scene iii, Line 35

Old men worry, and that prevents them from sleeping well.

'Tis the infirmity of his age; yet he hath ever but slenderly known himself.
Regan to Goneril
KING LEAR
Act I, Scene i, Line 292

His actions are the consequence of deterioration due to age. In addition, he has never been aware of what he truly was like.

Thou shouldst not have been old till thou hadst been wise.
Fool to Lear
KING LEAR
Act I, Scene v, Line 38

You should have become wise before you got old.

Age (cont'd)

The younger rises when the old doth fall.

Edmund in soliloquy
KING LEAR
Act III, Scene iii, Line 23

Youth inherits the power when the older generation succumbs to the frailties of age.

The oldest hath borne most; we that are young Shall never see so much, nor live so long.

Edgar to all
KING LEAR
Act V, Scene iii, Line 326

The oldest people have been burdened with the most trying experiences. We young people will never experience so much nor live as long.

Though age from folly could not give me freedom, It does from childishness.

Cleopatra to Antony
ANTONY AND CLEOPATRA
Act I, Scene iii, Line 57

Although becoming a mature adult does not prevent me from being foolish sometimes; nonetheless, I no longer behave childishly.

Allure

**Age cannot wither her, nor custom stale
Her infinite variety. Other women cloy
The appetites they feed, but she makes hungry
Where most she satisfies.**

Enobarbus to Maecenas
ANTONY AND CLEOPATRA
Act II, Scene ii, Line 236

As she gets older she still appears young; nor do men get tired of her many moods. Other women satiate their lovers, but she makes men want ever more of her charms.

Ambition

**These days are dangerous.
Virtue is choked with foul ambition.**

Gloucester to the King
2 HENRY VI
Act III, Scene i, Line 142

The current political situation is hazardous because virtuous officials are overwhelmed by officials who are bent on enriching their pockets or increasing their power.

Ambition (cont'd)

> But 'tis a common proof
> That lowliness is young ambition's ladder,
> Whereto the climber upward turns his face;
> But when he once attains the upmost round,
> He then unto the ladder turns his back,
> Looks in the clouds, scorning the base degrees
> By which he did ascend.
>
> *Brutus in soliloquy*
> *JULIUS CAESAR*
> *Act II, Scene i, Line 21*

It has commonly been seen that humility is the posture assumed by ambitious men initially, but once they achieve power, arrogance replaces humility.

Striving to better, oft we mar what's well.

Duke of Albany to Goneril
KING LEAR
Act I, Scene iv, Line 337

Often when we try to improve a satisfactory situation, we make things worse.

Ambition (cont'd)

**I have no spur
To prick the sides of my intent, but only
Vaulting ambition.**

Macbeth, aside
MACBETH
Act I, Scene vii, Line 25

I have no justification for what I intend to do aside from an ambition to improve my status.

Anticipation

**All things that are
Are with more spirit chasèd than enjoyed.**

Gratiano to Salerio
MERCHANT OF VENICE
Act II, Scene vi, Line 12

The pursuit of a goal is more satisfying than actually accomplishing the goal.

The image of it gives me content already, and I trust it will grow to a most prosperous perfection.

Isabella to Duke
MEASURE FOR MEASURE
Act III, Scene i, Line 252

The scheme makes me feel better already, and I trust it will develop to a very useful result.

Anticipation (cont'd)

Things won are done; joy's soul lies in the doing.

Cressida in soliloquy
TROILUS AND CRESSIDA
Act I, Scene ii, Line 273

Any objective that is achieved loses its appeal. True pleasure comes from working toward the objective.

Apology

I cannot make you what amends I would,
Therefore accept such kindness as I can.

Richard to Elizabeth
RICHARD III
Act IV, Scene iv, Line 309

I cannot accommodate your wishes even though I would like to do so; therefore, be satisfied with what I can do for you.

Appearance

**There is a fair behavior in thee,
And though that nature with a beauteous wall
Doth oft close in pollution, yet of thee
I will believe thou hast a mind that suits
With this thy fair and outward character.**

Viola to Captain
TWELFTH NIGHT
Act I, Scene ii, Line 47

You are a handsome person, and although good looks often disguise a devious attitude, yet I will believe that your appearance and your mind are similar in nature.

**O place, O form,
How often dost thou with thy case, thy habit,
Wrench awe from fools, and tie the wiser souls
To thy false seeming!**

Angelo in soliloquy
MEASURE FOR MEASURE
Act II, Scene iv, Line 12

The trappings of great authority awe simple people and even cause wiser people to be drawn into improper actions.

Appearance (cont'd)

**O, what may man within him hide,
Though angel on the outward side!**

Duke in soliloquy
MEASURE FOR MEASURE
Act III, Scene ii, Line 254

It's amazing the evil characteristics that a man may harbor even though he appears to be an upright person. (This Shakespearean observation is a common human interest story that fairly frequently makes the news in current society. Neighbors are often quoted as saying, "He seemed to be a quiet, reasonable man.")

Appreciation

**That what we have we prize not to the worth
Whiles we enjoy it, but being lacked and lost,
Why, then we rack the value, then we find
The virtue that possession would not show us
Whiles it was ours.**

Friar to all
MUCH ADO ABOUT NOTHING
Act IV, Scene i, Line 216

We do not value someone or something while we have it, but as soon as we lose it we consider it at length and then realize the value.

Apprehension

In time I may believe, yet I mistrust.

> Bianca to Lucentio
> TAMING OF THE SHREW
> Act III, Scene i, Line 49

In the future, I may believe what you assert, but currently I am skeptical.

Who dares not stir by day must walk by night.

> Bastard to Elinor
> KING JOHN
> Act I, Scene i, Line 172

Someone who wants to perform an unobserved deed must do it in the dark of night rather than in the daytime. (The use of the word "dares" implies that the deed is not praiseworthy.)

I see a strange confession in thine eye.
Thou shak'st thy head, and hold'st it fear or sin
To speak a truth.

> Northumberland to Morton
> 2 HENRY IV
> Act I, Scene i, Line 94

I see apprehension in your appearance. You're shaking your head, and you believe it will be either fearful or sinful to tell what the true situation is.

Apprehension (cont'd)

**I have been troubled in my sleep this night,
But dawning day new comfort hath inspired.**
Titus to his sons
TITUS ANDRONICUS
Act II, Scene ii, Line 9

I had unpleasant dreams last night, but the dawning of the new day has made me feel much better.

**Between the acting of a dreadful thing
And the first motion, all the interim is
Like a phantasma or a hideous dream.**
Brutus in soliloquy
JULIUS CAESAR
Act II, Scene i, Line 63

Between the actual doing of a dreadful act and the first thought of it is an interim period that's like an hallucination or a terrible dream.

Attitude

**There is nothing
either good or bad but thinking makes it so.**
Hamlet to R & G
HAMLET
Act II, Scene ii, Line 246

The way a situation is viewed depends on the attitude of the person involved.

Awareness

**As the morning steals upon the night,
Melting the darkness, so their rising senses
Begin to chase the ignorant fumes that mantle
Their clearer reason.**

Prospero to Ariel
THE TEMPEST
Act V, Scene i, Line 65

Just as the morning dispels the darkness, so they are
overcoming the ignorance that prevents them from
reasoning clearly.

Baldness

**There's no time for a man to recover his hair
that grows bald by nature.**

Dromio S. to Antipholus S.
COMEDY OF ERRORS
Act II, Scene ii, Line 71

There's no way to reverse the natural process of a man
becoming bald.

Beauty

Beauty provoketh thieves sooner than gold.
Rosalind to Celia
AS YOU LIKE IT
Act I, Scene iii, Line 106

Beautiful women attract malefactors more readily than money does.

Beauty is a witch
Against whose charms faith melteth into blood.
Claudio in soliloquy
MUCH ADO ABOUT NOTHING
Act II, Scene i, Line 161

When a beautiful woman is involved, the friendship between two men dissolves due to the drive of passion.

'Tis beauty truly blent, whose red and white
Nature's own sweet and cunning hand laid on.
Viola to Olivia
TWELFTH NIGHT
Act I, Scene v, Line 225

You are truly beautiful, and your natural coloring has been skillfully applied by Nature.

Beauty (cont'd)

Your beauty was the cause of that effect–
Your beauty that did haunt me in my sleep
To undertake the death of all the world
So I might live one hour in your sweet bosom.

Richard to Anne
RICHARD III
Act I, Scene ii, Line 121

Your beauty caused me to take that action. Your beauty obsessed me to the point that I would have killed everyone on earth if that would have allowed me to make love to you.

One fairer than my love? The all-seeing sun
Ne'er saw her match since first the world begun.

Romeo to Benvolio
ROMEO AND JULIET
Act I, Scene ii, Line 94

You say there are women more beautiful than the one I love? Not true, since she is the most beautiful woman that ever lived.

𝔅eauty (cont'd)

O, she doth teach the torches to burn bright!
It seems she hangs upon the cheek of night
Like a rich jewel in an Ethiop's ear –
Beauty too rich for use, for earth too dear!
So shows a snowy dove trooping with crows
As yonder lady o'er her fellows shows.

Romeo to Servingman
ROMEO AND JULIET
Act I, Scene v, Line 43

Her beauty is so great that it shines more brilliantly than torches. She stands out in the dark like a brilliant jewel worn by a dark person. Her beauty is extremely precious. Compared to other women she stands out like a white dove mixed in with black crows. (An Ethiopian, often shortened to "Ethiop," was the name Shakespeare normally used for a very dark-skinned person. Note Shakespeare's use of several similes in a sequence.)

O my love!
Death, that hath sucked the honey of thy breath,
Hath had no power yet upon thy beauty.
Thou art not conquered. Beauty's ensign yet
Is crimson in thy lips and in thy cheeks,
And death's pale flag is not advancèd there.

Romeo to Juliet
ROMEO AND JULIET
Act V, Scene iii, Line 91

O my love! Although death has stopped your breathing, your beauty is as yet unchanged.

Beauty (cont'd)

The beauty that is borne here in the face
The bearer knows not, but commends itself
To others' eyes.

Achilles to Ulysses
TROILUS AND CRESSIDA
Act III, Scene iii, Line 103

Beauty is in the eye of the beholder, not perceived by the person who is seen to be attractive by others.

Behavior

'Tis no time to jest,
And therefore frame your manners to the time.

Lucentio to Biondello
TAMING OF THE SHREW
Act I, Scene i, Line 222

Do not try to be amusing; the situation calls for a more serious. demeanor.

Blessing

**God bless thee; and put meekness in thy breast,
Love, charity, obedience, and true duty!**
Duchess of York to Richard
RICHARD III
Act II, Scene ii, Line 107

God bless you, and I charge you to be humble, loving, charitable, obedient, and to conduct yourself with faithfulness.

Bombast

**Here's a large mouth, indeed,
That spits forth death and mountains, rocks and seas;
Talks as familiarly of roaring lions
As maids of thirteen do of puppy-dogs!**
Bastard to all
KING JOHN
Act II, Scene i, Line 457

Listen to this loudmouth who talks about death and mountains, rocks and seas. He talks as casually about roaring lions as little girls talk about puppies.

Bore

> **O, he is as tedious**
> **As a tired horse, a railing wife;**
> **Worse than a smoky house. I had rather live**
> **With cheese and garlic in a windmill far**
> **Than feed on cates and have him talk to me**
> **In any summer house in Christendom.**
>
> *Hotspur to Mortimer*
> *1 HENRY IV*
> *Act III, Scene i, Line 157*

Oh, he is as annoying as riding a tired horse or listening to a nagging wife, and he is worse than a smoky house. I would rather live with meager food in isolation than to eat delicacies and have to listen to him in pleasant surroundings.

Caution

> **Advantage is a better soldier than rashness.**
>
> *Montjoy to Henry V*
> *HENRY V*
> *Act III, Scene vi, Line 115*

In war, caution is more advantageous than rashness.

Caution (cont'd)

**Heat not a furnace for your foe so hot
That it do singe yourself.**

Norfolk to Buckingham
HENRY VIII
Act I, Scene i, Line 140

Do not put so much effort into creating a situation that is detrimental to your enemy if it hurts you as well.

Wisely, and slow. They stumble that run fast.

Friar to Romeo
ROMEO AND JULIET
Act II, Scene iii, Line 94

Lack of caution causes mishaps and misunderstandings.

**Modest doubt is called
The beacon of the wise.**

Hector to Priam
TROILUS AND CRESSIDA
Act II, Scene ii, Line 15

Moderate doubt is known as a guide to a prudent person.

Chance

**If Hercules and Lichas play at dice
Which is the better man, the greater throw
May turn by fortune from the weaker hand.**
Morocco to Portia
MERCHANT OF VENICE
Act II, Scene i, Line 32

Pure chance does not respect strength.

Chaos

**The times are wild. Contention, like a horse
Full of high feeding, madly hath broke loose
And bears down all before him.**
Northumberland to Bardolf
2 HENRY IV
Act I, Scene i, Line 9

There is great social disorder. People are fighting against one another and many are being killed.

Character

**Is not birth, beauty, good shape, discourse, manhood,
learning, gentleness, virtue, youth, liberality,
and such like, the spice and salt that season a man?**

Pandarus to Cressida
TROILUS AND CRESSIDA
Act I, Scene ii, Line 239

Are not birth, beauty, good shape, etc., the attributes that give a man character?

Charity

**Take physic, pomp;
Expose thyself to feel what wretches feel,
That thou mayst shake the superflux to them
And show the heavens more just.**

Lear in soliloquy
KING LEAR
Act III, Scene iv, Line 33

Cure yourselves, you vainglorious ones; expose yourself to the problems of the poor in order to incline you to share some of your riches, thereby making them feel there is some justice.

Cheerfulness

Though news be sad, yet tell them merrily;
If good, thou shamest the music of sweet news
By playing it to me with so sour a face.

Juliet to Nurse
ROMEO AND JULIET
Act II, Scene v, Line 22

Even though the news you bring is sad, please present it pleasantly. If your news is good, you distort it by reporting it with such a grim demeanor.

Choice

Faith, as you say, there's small choice in rotten apples.

Hortensio to Gremio
TAMING OF THE SHREW
Act I, Scene i, Line 132

There's little choice between undesirable alternatives.

I am in blood
Stepped in so far that, should I wade no more,
Returning were as tedious as go o'er.

Macbeth to Lady Macbeth
MACBETH
Act III, Scene iv, Line 136

I am so deeply involved that if I stopped and tried to retract my actions, it would be as tiring as to continue.

Cleverness

**This rudeness is a sauce to his good wit,
Which gives men stomach to digest his words
With better appetite.**
Cassius to Brutus
JULIUS CAESAR
Act I, Scene ii, Line 297

His caustic manner is an ornament to display his intelligence, which has the effect of getting others to listen to him and enjoy what he is saying.

Comfort

**Comfort's in heaven, and we are on the earth,
Where nothing lives but crosses, cares, and grief.**
York to the Queen
RICHARD II
Act II, Scene ii, Line 78

There is comfort in heaven, but we are on earth and we encounter nothing but thwartings, cares, and grief.

Compulsion

Give you a reason on compulsion? If reasons were as plentiful as blackberries, I would give no man a reason upon compulsion, I.

Falstaff to Prince Hal
1 HENRY IV
Act II, Scene iv, Line 227

Explain my actions because you demand it? Even if explanations were exceedingly plentiful, I would give no man an explanation because he demanded it.

Confidence

**The eagle suffers little birds to sing,
And is not careful what they mean thereby,
Knowing that with the shadow of his wings
He can at pleasure stint their melody.**

Tamora to Saturnius
TITUS ANDRONICUS
Act IV, Scene iv, Line 82

A powerful person is not concerned by the activities of powerless people since he knows that he can restrain them at his pleasure.

Conflict

**Where two raging fires meet together
They do consume the thing that feeds their fury.**

*Petruchio to Baptista
TAMING OF THE SHREW
Act II, Scene i, Line 132*

When two headstrong personalities interact, they come to an accommodation. (Not often in real life, to be sure, but this is the fundamental assertion of "The Taming of the Shrew.")

Confusion

**Brief as the lightning in the collied night,
That, in a spleen, unfolds both heaven and earth,
And ere a man hath power to say 'Behold!'
The jaws of darkness do devour it up:
So quick bright things come to confusion.**

*Lysander to Hermia
MIDSUMMER NIGHT'S DREAM
Act I, Scene i, Line 145*

The duration of a pleasant experience, such as youthful love, often is short-lived and can be compared to a flash of lightning in the darkness of night.

Confusion (cont'd)

His speech was like a tangled chain; nothing impaired, but all disordered.

Theseus to all
MIDSUMMER NIGHT'S DREAM
Act IV, Scene i, Line 124

His speech contained all the appropriate words, but the sequence was confusing.

Conscience

Let not our babbling dreams affright our souls;
Conscience is but a word that cowards use,
Devised at first to keep the strong in awe.
Our strong arms be our conscience, swords our law!
March on, join bravely, let us to it pell-mell;
If not to heaven, then hand in hand to hell.

Richard to Norfolk
RICHARD III
Act V, Scene iii, Line 309

Do not let meaningless dreams frighten us. Conscience is only a word that cowards invoke to deter strong foes. Let our strength and arms be our conscience and law. Let us go to battle together forcefully, and if we don't get to heaven, then we'll be together in hell.

Conscience (cont'd)

**Unnatural deeds
Do breed unnatural troubles. Infected minds
To their deaf pillows will discharge their secrets.**

Doctor to Gentlewoman
MACBETH
Act V, Scene i, Line 66

Terrible misdeeds create strange mental problems. Anguished minds will talk in their sleep.

Consideration

I have no superfluous leisure; my stay must be stolen out of other affairs, but I will attend you a while.

Isabella to Duke
MEASURE FOR MEASURE
Act III, Scene i, Line 157

I have no spare time. My remaining here takes time away from other duties, but I will wait a while at your request.

Consolation

**Thou bring'st me happiness and peace,
But health, alack, with youthful wings is flown
From this bare withered trunk. Upon thy sight
My worldly business makes a period.**

King Henry to Prince Hal
2 HENRY IV
Act IV, Scene v, Line 227

Your arrival has brought me happiness and peace, but my health is gone with my youth. Now that you're here, I will die.

Contrition

Happy are they that hear their detractions and can put them to mending.

Benedict in soliloquy
MUCH ADO ABOUT NOTHING
Act II, Scene iii, Line 210

It is very beneficial for someone who learns of his or her faults and then acts to correct them.

Coolness

**When love begins to sicken and decay
It useth an enforcèd ceremony.
There are no tricks in plain and simple faith.**

Brutus to Lucilius
JULIUS CAESAR
Act IV, Scene ii, Line 20

When a friend loses his enthusiasm for another, the tone of the response becomes formal, whereas a genuine friendship is simple and straight-forward.

Courage

A heart unspotted is not easily daunted.

Gloucester to Suffolk
2 HENRY VI
Act III, Scene i, Line 100

A person who is not guilty is not easily frightened.

Courage (cont'd)

**Let not our babbling dreams affright our souls;
Conscience is but a word that cowards use,
Devised at first to keep the strong in awe.
Our strong arms be our conscience, swords our law!
March on, join bravely, let us to it pell-mell;
If not to heaven, then hand in hand to hell.**

Richard to Norfolk
RICHARD III
Act V, Scene iii, Line 309

Do not let meaningless dreams frighten us. Conscience is only
a word that cowards invoke to deter strong foes. Let our strength
and arms be our conscience and law. Let us go to battle
together forcefully, and if we don't get to heaven, then we'll
be together in hell.

**But I must go and meet with danger there,
Or it will seek me in another place
And find me worse provided.**

Northumberland to Lady Percy
2 HENRY IV
Act II, Scene iii, Line 48

If I don't go and face danger at that location, I'll encounter it
somewhere else, at which point I'll be less prepared to
deal with it.

Courage (cont'd)

I dare do all that may become a man;
Who dares do more is none.

> *Macbeth to Lady Macbeth*
> *MACBETH*
> *Act I, Scene vii, Line 46*

I am willing to attempt all that is appropriate for a man to do.
He who will do more than that is not a true man.

We fail?
But screw your courage to the sticking-place
And we'll not fail.

> *Lady Macbeth to Macbeth*
> *MACBETH*
> *Act I, Scene vii, Line 59*

We fail? Just be very courageous and we'll not fail.

The mind I sway by and the heart I bear
Shall never sag with doubt nor shake with fear.

> *Macbeth to all*
> *MACBETH*
> *Act V, Scene iii, Line 9*

My determination and my courage will never falter.

Courage (cont'd)

**Nay, good my fellows, do not please sharp fate
To grace it with your sorrows. Bid that welcome
Which comes to punish us, and we punish it,
Seeming to bear it lightly.**

Antony to all
ANTONY AND CLEOPATRA
Act IV, Scene xiv, Line 135

No, my friends, do not let hard fortune be pleased to hear your lamentations. Rather, accept the consequences readily, and we'll punish fortune by our apparent unconcern.

Courtship

These fellows of infinite tongue, that can rhyme themselves into ladies' favors, they do always reason themselves out again.

Henry V to Katherine
HENRY V
Act V, Scene ii, Line 154

These garrulous men who can speak poetically to win the love of women later figure out how to avoid involvement.

Cowardice

Cowards die many times before their deaths;
The valiant never taste of death but once.

Caesar to Calphurnia
JULIUS CAESAR
Act II, Scene ii, Line 32

Because of their fear of death, cowards have the sensation of death many times, but valiant people only face death when they actually die.

Curses

Some devil whisper curses in my ear,
And prompt me that my tongue may utter forth
The venomous malice of my swelling heart!

Aaron to all
TITUS ANDRONICUS
Act V, Scene iii, Line 11

Some devil whisper curses in my ear to prompt me so that I can speak the nasty hatred flowing from my angry feelings.

Curses (cont'd)

The common curse of mankind, folly and ignorance, be thine in great revenue!

Thersites to Patroclus
TROILUS AND CRESSIDA
Act II, Scene iii, Line 25

The common curse of mankind, folly and ignorance, be yours in great abundance.

Cycles

**Thus sometimes hath the brightest day a cloud,
And after summer evermore succeeds
Barren winter with his wrathful nipping cold;
So cares and joys abound, as seasons fleet.**

Glouster to all
2 HENRY VI
Act II, Scene iv, Line 1

Life is a series of ups and downs. (A common Shakespearean observation.)

Danger

**These days are dangerous.
Virtue is choked with foul ambition.**

*Gloucester to the King
2 HENRY VI
Act III, Scene i, Line 142*

The current political situation is hazardous because virtuous officials are overwhelmed by officials who are bent on enriching their pockets or increasing their power.

**This spark will prove a raging fire
If wind and fuel be brought to feed it with.**

*Queen to York
2 HENRY VI
Act III, Scene i, Line 302*

Self-evident on its face, but it is intended to apply to a political incident and the subsequent actions.

**But I must go and meet with danger there,
Or it will seek me in another place
And find me worse provided.**

*Northumberland to Lady Percy
2 HENRY IV
Act II, Scene iii, Line 48*

If I don't go and face danger at that location, I'll encounter it somewhere else, at which point I'll be less prepared to deal with it.

Danger (cont'd)

**These violent delights have violent ends
And in their triumph die, like fire and powder,
Which, as they kiss, consume.**
Friar to Romeo
ROMEO AND JULIET
Act II, Scene vi, Line 9

Intense pleasures, especially those of love, result in
catastrophes similar to the action of igniting (gun)powder.

**Into what dangers would you lead me,
That you would have me seek into myself
For that which is not in me?**
Brutus to Cassius
JULIUS CAESAR
Act I, Scene ii, Line 63

What are you trying to get me involved with that you are
suggesting I examine my convictions to find an attitude
that I don't think I have?

**Think him as a serpent's egg
Which hatched would as his kind grow mischievous,
And kill him in the shell.**
Brutus in soliloquy
JULIUS CAESAR
Act II, Scene i, Line 32

Justify political murder on the basis that, although the adversary
is powerless now, he will develop despotic powers in the future.

Danger (cont'd)

> Alas, what shall I say?
> My credit now stands on such slippery ground,
> That one of two bad ways you must conceit me,
> Either a coward or a flatterer.
>
> *Antony to all*
> *JULIUS CAESAR*
> *Act III, Scene i, Line 191*

How can I defend myself? I'm in a very awkward situation inasmuch as if I don't stand opposed to you, I will appear either as a coward or to be pandering to you.

Death

Grim death, how foul and loathsome is thy image!

Lord to Huntsman
TAMING OF THE SHREW
Induction, Scene i, Line 33

The sight of a dead person is terrible to behold.

And may not young men die as well as old?

Gremio to Tranio
TAMING OF THE SHREW
Act II, Scene i, Line 393

Isn't it possible for young men to die as well as old men? (Another one of the many places where Shakespeare reminds us of the dangers of life.)

Death (cont'd)

The sense of death is most in apprehension.
Isabella to Claudio
MEASURE FOR MEASURE
Act III, Scene i, Line 78

The fear and awareness of death is felt primarily as a sense of apprehension of its occurrence.

**The weariest and most loathèd worldly life
That age, ache, penury, and imprisonment
Can lay on nature is a paradise
To what we fear of death.**
Claudio to Isabella
MEASURE FOR MEASURE
Act III, Scene i, Line 129

The worst life we can imagine is marvelous compared to what we fear that death will be like.

**That life is better life, past fearing death,
Than that which lives to fear.**
Duke to Isabella
MEASURE FOR MEASURE
Act V, Scene i, Line 393

Life is better after it acknowledges the death of a loved one, rather than if lived in fear of imminent death.

Death (cont'd)

**Just Death, kind umpire of men's miseries,
With sweet enlargement doth dismiss me hence.**
Mortimer to Jailer
1 HENRY VI
Act II, Scene v, Line 29

Just Death, which ends the misery of life, gives me freedom by ending my life.

**But kings and mightiest potentates must die,
For that's the end of human misery.**
Talbot to Burgundy
1 HENRY VI
Act III, Scene ii, Line 136

The high and the low all share the same end: Death.

**Ah, what a sign it is of evil life
Where death's approach is seen so terrible.**
King to the Cardinal
2 HENRY VI
Act III, Scene iii, Line 5

The fact that a person reacts to the imminence of death with great foreboding is an indication that he or she fears retribution for the evil life he or she has lived.

Death (cont'd)

O thou eternal Mover of the heavens,
Look with gentle eye upon this wretch.
O, beat away the busy meddling fiend
That lays strong siege unto this wretch's soul,
And from his bosom purge this black despair.
King to God
2 HENRY VI
Act III, Scene iii, Line 19

Oh God, be merciful to this miserable man and purge from him the devil that attacks his soul and take away the terrible despair he feels.

There is so hot a summer in my bosom
That all my bowels crumble up to dust.
I am a scribbled form drawn with a pen
Upon a parchment, and against this fire
Do I shrink up.
John to all
KING JOHN
Act V, Scene vii, Line 30

I have such a terrible fever that I feel as if my guts are turning to dust. I am like a sketch on a piece of paper, which, when the paper burns, shrivels up.

Death (cont'd)

The tackle of my heart is cracked and burnt,
And all the shrouds wherewith my life should sail
Are turned to one thread, one little hair.
> *John to Bastard*
> *KING JOHN*
> *Act V, Scene vii, Line 52*

The sinews of my heart are very deteriorated, and all the inner mechanisms that support life are weakened to the point of being no stronger than one small thread.

O, but they say that the tongues of dying men
Enforce attention like deep harmony.
> *Gaunt to York*
> *RICHARD II*
> *Act II, Scene i, Line 5*

Oh, but they say that words spoken by dying men make people listen as does impressive music.

More are men's ends marked than their lives before.
> *Gaunt to York*
> *RICHARD II*
> *Act II, Scene i, Line 11*

What men say at the end of their lives is noted more carefully than that which they say during their lives.

Death (cont'd)

**Even through the hollow eyes of death
I spy life peering.**

*Northumberland to Ross
RICHARD II
Act II, Scene i, Line 270*

Even in a deadly situation I see the possibility of improvement or renewal.

**Cry woe, destruction, ruin, and decay:
The worst is death, and death will have his day.**

*King Richard to all
RICHARD II
Act III, Scene ii, Line 102*

When considering the disasters of woe, destruction, ruin, and decay, even these are surpassed by death and death eventually arrives in any event.

Peace! Do not speak like a death's-head. Do not bid me remember mine end.

*Falstaff to Doll
2 HENRY IV
Act II, Scene iv, Line 217*

Be quiet. Do not talk as if you are the grim reaper. Do not ask me to remember that one day I will die.

Death (cont'd)

Thou bring'st me happiness and peace,
But health, alack, with youthful wings is flown
From this bare withered trunk. Upon thy sight
My worldly business makes a period.
King Henry to Prince Hal
2 HENRY IV
Act IV, Scene v, Line 227

Your arrival has brought me happiness and peace, but my health is gone with my youth. Now that you're here, I will die.

In peace and honor rest you here, my sons;
Secure from worldly chances and mishaps.
Here lurks no treason, here no envy swells,
Here grow no damnèd drugs, here are no storms,
No noise, but silence and eternal sleep.
Titus to all
TITUS ANDRONICUS
Act I, Scene i, Line 153

Rest in your graves, my sons, secure from life's uncertain events. Here there are none of life's tribulations, but only silence and eternal sleep.

𝔇eath (cont'd)

> **O my love!**
> **Death, that hath sucked the honey of thy breath,**
> **Hath had no power yet upon thy beauty.**
> **Thou art not conquered. Beauty's ensign yet**
> **Is crimson in thy lips and in thy cheeks,**
> **And death's pale flag is not advancèd there.**
>
> *Romeo to Juliet*
> *ROMEO AND JULIET*
> *Act V, Scene iii, Line 91*

O my love! Although death has stopped your breathing, your beauty is as yet unchanged.

> **Thou know'st 'tis common. All that lives must die,**
> **Passing through nature to eternity.**
>
> *Gertrude to Hamlet*
> *HAMLET*
> *Act I, Scene ii, Line 72*

You know that it is a normal part of life. Everything that lives must die, passing through a mortal stage to eternity.

𝔇eath (cont'd)

**To die, to sleep–
To sleep–perchance to dream: ay, there's the rub,
For in that sleep of death what dreams may come
When we have shuffled off this mortal coil,
Must give us pause.**

Hamlet in soliloquy
HAMLET
Act III, Scene i, Line 64

The thought of a quiet, peaceful, sleeping death is appealing until we consider what painful dreams we might have. This makes us hesitate.

**Vex not his ghost. O, let him pass! He hates him
That would upon the rack of this tough world
Stretch him out longer.**

Kent to Edgar
KING LEAR
Act V, Scene iii, Line 314

Let him die. He would be angry towards anyone who would want to prolong his life in this hard cruel world.

Death (cont'd)

> **Nothing in his life**
> **Became him like the leaving it. He died**
> **As one that had been studied in his death,**
> **To throw away the dearest thing he owed**
> **As 'twere a careless trifle.**
>
> *Malcom to Duncan*
> *MACBETH*
> *Act I, Scene iv, Line 7*

Nothing he did during his life was as admirable as the way he died. He approached his death fearlessly and seemed willing to lose it as if it mattered very little to him.

> **The sleeping and the dead**
> **Are but as pictures; 'tis the eye of childhood**
> **That fears a painted devil.**
>
> *Lady Macbeth to Macbeth*
> *MACBETH*
> *Act II, Scene ii, Line 52*

People who are sleeping or dead are simply like pictures. It takes the imagination of a child to be fearful of a picture of a frightening-looking devil.

𝔇𝔢𝔞𝔱𝔥 (cont'd)

Tomorrow, and tomorrow, and tomorrow
Creeps in this petty pace from day to day
To the last syllable of recorded time;
And all our yesterdays have lighted fools
The way to dusty death.
Macbeth to Seyton
MACBETH
Act V, Scene v, Line 19

The future slowly comes on a day-to-day basis until the end of time. The past has been simply a process in which foolish people have gone to their deaths.

Out, out, brief candle!
Life's but a walking shadow, a poor player
That struts and frets his hour upon the stage
And then is heard no more.
Macbeth to Seyton
MACBETH
Act V, Scene v, Line 23

End, brief life. Life's nothing but an intangible essence that appears on earth for a short time and then is no longer heard from.

Death (cont'd)

Death may usurp on nature many hours,
And yet the fire of life kindle again
The o'erpressed spirits.

Cerimon to all
PERICLES
Act III, Scene ii, Line 81

A deathlike coma may take much time from living, but recovery may still be achieved.

Now our sands are almost run;
More a little, and then dumb.

Gower, as Chorus
PERICLES
Act V, Scene ii, Line 1

The time for our play is almost over. Just a little more time, and then we will be silent. (Also applies to old age, of course.)

By med'cine life may be prolonged, yet death
Will seize the doctor too.

Cymbeline to Cornelius
CYMBELINE
Act V, Scene v, Line 29

Although we may extend life for a while by giving a person medicine for his or her illness, death is seen to be inevitable in that even the knowledgeable person who can dispense medicine to extend life will him or herself die.

Death (cont'd)

He that dies pays all debts.
Stefano to Trinculo
THE TEMPEST
Act III, Scene ii, Line 128

Death is the payment of the ultimate debt.

We are such stuff
As dreams are made on, and our little life
Is rounded with a sleep.
Prospero to Ferdinand
THE TEMPEST
Act IV, Scene i, Line 156

We humans are as ephemeral as dreams, and our short life on earth is preceded by nothing and is followed by nothing.

Deceit

Things are often spoke and seldom meant.
Suffolk to the King
2 HENRY VI
Act III, Scene i, Line 268

Duplicity is common.

Deceit (cont'd)

'Tis time to fear when tyrants seem to kiss.
Pericles to Helicanus
PERICLES
Act I, Scene ii, Line 78

Be suspicious when tyrants appear to treat you well.

Who makes the fairest show means most deceit.
Cleon to a Lord
PERICLES
Act I, Scene iv, Line 75

Those who make an ostentatious effort of treating you well intend to cause you harm.

No visor does become black villainy
So well as soft and tender flattery.
Gower, as Chorus
PERICLES
Act IV, Scene iv, Line 44

No deceptive appearance serves nefarious intentions as well as flattering words.

Deception

**In religion,
What damnèd error but some sober brow
Will bless it and approve it with a text,
Hiding the grossness with fair ornament?**

Bassanio to himself and Portia
MERCHANT OF VENICE
Act III, Scene ii, Line 77

When it comes to religion, a clear sin may be rationalized by some serious-looking authority who quotes a passage from the scriptures, thereby obscuring the reality by means of elegant words.

**The pleasant'st angling is to see the fish
Cut with her golden oars the silver stream
And greedily devour the treacherous bait.**

Ursula to Hero
MUCH ADO ABOUT NOTHING
Act III, Scene i, Line 26

It is rewarding sport to watch a fish break through the surface of the water as it grasps for the bait. (Or, as is the case in the play where this line is used, it is great sport to fool someone with a false story and to watch them become convinced it is true.)

Deception (cont'd)

Some Cupid kills with arrows, some with traps.

Hero to Ursula
MUCH ADO ABOUT NOTHING
Act III, Scene i, Line 106

Sometimes love comes at first sight, but in other cases it is necessary to use devious means to engender love.

These fellows of infinite tongue, that can rhyme themselves into ladies' favors, they do always reason themselves out again.

Henry V to Katherine
HENRY V
Act V, Scene ii, Line 154

These garrulous men who can speak poetically to win the love of women figure out later how to avoid involvement.

Affairs that walk—
As they say spirits do—at midnight, have
In them a wilder nature than the business
That seeks dispatch by day.

Gardiner to Lovell
HENRY VIII
Act V, Scene i, Line 13

Affairs that are conducted late at night have a more pressing nature than those that are conducted in the daytime.

Deception (cont'd)

**Good gentlemen, look fresh and merrily;
Let not our looks put on our purposes.**

Brutus to all
JULIUS CAESAR
Act II, Scene i, Line 224

Good gentlemen, appear bright and merry; don't let your appearances expose our purposes.

**Let us, like merchants, show our foulest wares
And think perchance they'll sell; if not, the luster
Of the better yet to show shall show the better,
By showing the worst first.**

Ulysses to Nestor
TROILUS AND CRESSIDA
Act I, Scene iii, Line 358

Let us, acting as if we were merchants, present our least acceptable proposals first, hoping to have them agreed to. If not, then our more attractive proposals will appear much better by comparison.

𝔇𝔢𝔠𝔢𝔭𝔱𝔦𝔬𝔫 (cont'd)

When my outward action doth demonstrate
The native act and figure of my heart
In compliment extern, 'tis not long after
But I will wear my heart upon my sleeve
For daws to peck at; I am not what I am.

Iago to Roderigo
OTHELLO
Act I, Scene i, Line 61

When my apparent actions are consistent with what I really intend, I might as well be as foolish as to wear my heart on my sleeve for birds to eat. My true intentions are not what they appear to be.

Though I do hate him as I do hell-pains,
Yet, for necessity of present life,
I must show out a flag and sign of love,
Which is indeed but sign.

Iago to Roderigo
OTHELLO
Act I, Scene i, Line 153

Although I hate him very much, because of the current situation I must make it appear that I admire him, but this is only put on.

Deception (cont'd)

> **'Tis here, but yet confused;**
> **Knavery's plain face is never seen till used.**
>
> *Iago in soliloquy*
> OTHELLO
> *Act II, Scene i, Line 305*

My nefarious scheme is forming in my mind, but it is not yet clear. It won't be entirely clear until it's actually implemented.

> **When devils will the blackest sins put on,**
> **They do suggest at first with heavenly shows**
>
> *Iago in soliloquy*
> OTHELLO
> *Act II, Scene iii, Line 334*

When evil people intend to do very villainous deeds, they disguise their intent with very righteous appearances.

> **But, 'tis strange**
> **And oftentimes, to win us to our harm,**
> **The instruments of darkness tell us truths,**
> **Win us with honest trifles, to betray's**
> **In deepest consequence.**
>
> *Banquo to Macbeth*
> MACBETH
> *Act I, Scene iii, Line 122*

It's difficult to perceive, but oftentimes the forces of evil deceive us with trivial truths (or our own rationalizations), only to lead us to disaster in later developments.

𝔇𝔢𝔠𝔢𝔭𝔱𝔦𝔬𝔫 (cont'd)

There's no art
To find the mind's construction in the face.

Duncan to all
MACBETH
Act I, Scene iv, Line 11

There is no method by which one can determine what a person really thinks by observing his facial expressions.

Stars, hide your fires;
Let not light see my black and deep desires.

Macbeth, aside
MACBETH
Act I, Scene iv, Line 50

Stars, do not shine. Let no light reveal my sinister intentions.

Your face is as a book where men
May read strange matters. To beguile the time,
Look like the time; bear welcome in your eye,
Your hand, your tongue; look like the innocent flower,
But be the serpent under't.

Lady Macbeth to Macbeth
MACBETH
Act I, Scene v, Line 60

The look on your face makes it apparent that you are concerned with unusual considerations. To deceive those around you, project a pleasant and innocent appearance, but be prepared to attack at the right opportunity.

Deception (cont'd)

False face must hide what the false heart doth know.
Lady Macbeth to Macbeth
MACBETH
Act I, Scene vii, Line 81

A deceptive appearance must be a cover for evil intentions.

To show an unfelt sorrow is an office
Which the false man does easy.
Malcom to Donalbain
MACBETH
Act II, Scene iii, Line 132

To feign sorrow is a role that a deceitful man performs well.

Decline

Farewell!
I have touched the highest point of all my greatness,
And from that full meridian of my glory
I haste now to my setting.
Wosley in soliloquy
HENRY VIII
Act III, Scene ii, Line 222

Good-bye! I have risen to the pinnacle of my career, and I now am going to sink into oblivion.

Decline (cont'd)

**Now does he feel his title
Hang loose about him, like a giant's robe
Upon a dwarfish thief.**
Angus to all
MACBETH
Act V, Scene ii, Line 20

Now he feels that his high position is too great for his
low stature.

**When Fortune in her shift and change of mood
Spurns down her late beloved, all his dependents,
Which labored after him to the mountain's top
Even on their knees and hands, let him slip down,
Not one accompanying his declining foot.**
Poet to Painter
TIMON OF ATHENS
Act I, Scene i, Line 84

When capricious fortune turns on a man, driving him from the heights
to the depths, those who followed him when he was ascending
do not remain faithful and assist him when he is descending.

Degradation

> **What is a man,**
> **If his chief good and market of his time**
> **Be but to sleep and feed? A beast, no more.**
>
> *Hamlet in soliloquy*
> *HAMLET*
> *Act IV, Scene iv, Line 33*

What is the worth of a man if all he does is sleep and eat? None. He's no more than a beast.

Demagoguery

> **The reasons you allege do more conduce**
> **To the hot passion of distemp'red blood**
> **Than to make up a free determination**
> **'Twixt right and wrong; for pleasure and revenge**
> **Have ears more deaf than adders to the voice**
> **Of any true decision.**
>
> *Hector to Paris and Troilus*
> *TROILUS AND CRESSIDA*
> *Act II, Scene ii, Line 168*

The reasons that you are promoting apply more to influence an angry person than to make a calm evaluation between right and wrong. This is because self-satisfaction and the desire for revenge do not want to listen to careful reasoning leading to a logical decision.

Demise

**Thy rage shall burn thee up, and thou shalt turn
To ashes.**
Philip to John
KING JOHN
Act III, Scene ii, Line 344

Your rage shall cause your destruction.

Despair

**Oft expectation fails, and most oft there
Where most it promises; and oft it hits
Where hope is coldest, and despair most fits.**
Helena to King
ALL'S WELL THAT ENDS WELL
Act II, Scene i, Line 142

We often find that our expectations do not work out, especially
when it appears most likely they will; often our expectations
do work out when we least expect them to do so.

Despair (cont'd)

**There is so hot a summer in my bosom
That all my bowels crumble up to dust.
I am a scribbled form drawn with a pen
Upon a parchment, and against this fire
Do I shrink up.**

John to all
KING JOHN
Act V, Scene vii, Line 30

I have such a terrible fever that I feel as if my guts are turning to dust. I am like a sketch on a piece of paper, which, when the paper burns, shrivels up.

**The tackle of my heart is cracked and burnt,
And all the shrouds wherewith my life should sail
Are turned to one thread, one little hair.**

John to Bastard
KING JOHN
Act V, Scene vii, Line 52

The sinews of my heart are very deteriorated, and all the inner mechanisms that support life are weakened to the point of being no stronger than one small thread.

Desperation

> **I do spy a kind of hope,**
> **Which craves as desperate an execution**
> **As that is desperate which we would prevent.**
>
> *Friar to Juliet*
> *ROMEO AND JULIET*
> *Act IV, Scene i, Line 68*

I see a possible plan of action that requires a very desperate operation, which is comparable in danger to the desperate problem that is to be corrected.

> **Diseases desperate grown**
> **By desperate appliance are relieved,**
> **Or not at all.**
>
> *Claudius to all*
> *HAMLET*
> *Act IV, Scene iii, Line 9*

A disease which is seriously advanced can be helped by desperate measures, or else nothing can be done.

Despondency

> **There's nothing in this world can make me joy.**
> **Life is as tedious as a twice-told tale**
> **Vexing the dull ear of a drowsy man.**
>
> *Lewis to Pandulph*
> *KING JOHN*
> *Act III, Scene iv, Line 107*

There is nothing in the world that can make me happy.
Life is very boring.

Despondency (cont'd)

**I have a soul of lead
So stakes me to the ground I cannot move.**
Romeo to Mercutio
ROMEO AND JULIET
Act I, Scene iv, Line 15

I am so despondent I feel that I cannot move.

Devil

I think the devil will not have me damned, lest the oil that's in me should set hell on fire.
Falstaff in soliloquy
MERRY WIVES OF WINDSOR
Act V, Scene v, Line 32

I doubt the devil will damn me for fear my fat might set hell on fire. (Expression of hope by a fat miscreant man.)

Devotion

**When holy and devout religious men
Are at their beads, 'tis much to draw them thence,
So sweet is zealous contemplation.**
Buckingham to Mayor
RICHARD III
Act III, Scene vii, Line 92

When devout men are praying, it is difficult to disturb them.

Dilemma

**I am in blood
Stepped in so far that, should I wade more,
Returning were as tedious as go o'er.**
> *Macbeth to Lady Macbeth*
> *MACBETH*
> *Act III, Scene iv, Line 136*

I am so deeply involved that if I stopped and tried to retract
my actions, it would be as tiring as to continue.

Directness

An honest tale speeds best being plainly told.
> *Elizabeth to Richard*
> *RICHARD III*
> *Act IV, Scene iv, Line 358*

A true story is best understood by telling it simply.

**What need'st thou run so many miles about,
When thou mayest tell thy tale the nearest way?**
> *Richard to Stanley*
> *RICHARD III*
> *Act IV, Scene iv, Line 460*

Do not engage in circumlocution.

Directness (cont'd)

**I have neither wit, nor words, nor worth,
Action, nor utterance, nor the power of speech,
To stir men's blood. I only speak right on.**
Antony to all
JULIUS CAESAR
Act III, Scene ii, Line 221

I have neither the skill of inventions, nor fluency, nor public stature, skill of gesturing, nor elegant delivery, nor powerful words to incite men. I only speak straightforwardly, just as I think.

Believe me, I speak as my understanding instructs me and as mine honesty puts it to utterance.
Archidamus to Camillo
WINTER'S TALE
Act I, Scene i, Line 18

Believe me, I speak according to my understanding of the circumstances and I say it as truthfully as I can.

Disappointment

Things sweet to taste prove in digestion sour.
Gaunt to King Richard
RICHARD II
Act I, Scene iii, Line 236

Actions or ideas that seem good at first turn out to be bad after living with them for a while.

Disappointment (cont'd)

**The ample proposition that hope makes
In all designs begun on earth below
Fails in the promised largeness. Checks and disasters
Grow in the veins of actions highest reared.**

Agamemnon to all
TROILUS AND CRESSIDA
Act I, Scene iii, Line 3

The great good hoped for from programs engaged in by humans does not occur as expected because problems are inherent in even the most exalted of human efforts.

**O you gods!
Why do you make us love your goodly gifts
And snatch them straight away?**

Pericles to the Gods
PERICLES
Act III, Scene i, Line 22

Oh you gods! Why do you teach us to love your gifts and then make us lose them? (Applied in the play with regard to the death of a loved one.)

Disdain

**Disdain and scorn ride sparkling in her eyes,
Misprizing what they look on; and her wit
Values itself so highly that to her
All matter else seems weak.**

Hero to Ursula
MUCH ADO ABOUT NOTHING
Act III, Scene i, Line 51

She so highly values her own intelligence that she disdains all others and any emotional matters (such as love) are unimportant to her.

**What's the matter, you dissentious rogues,
That, rubbing the poor itch of your opinion,
Make yourselves scabs?**

Marcius to crowd
CORIOLANUS
Act I, Scene i, Line 159

What's your complaint, you seditious rogues, that by expressing your inconsequential opinions, you invent miseries?

Disgrace

> Like a dull actor now
> I have forgot my part and I am out,
> Even to a full disgrace.
>
> *Coriolanus to Virgilia*
> *CORIOLANUS*
> *Act V, Scene iii, Line 40*

I have forgotten my true role in life and therefore I am disgraced.

Dissemblance

> O dissembling courtesy! How fine this tyrant
> Can tickle where she wounds!
>
> *Imogen to Posthumas*
> *CYMBELINE*
> *Act I, Scene i, Line 84*

Oh disguised politeness. How well this powerful artifice can pretend to gratify while actually doing damage.

Dissipation

> You are as a candle, the better part burnt out.
>
> *Chief Justice to Falstaff*
> *2 HENRY IV*
> *Act I, Scene ii, Line 148*

You are like a candle, of which the best part has been used up.

Distinction

In the wind and tempest of her frown
Distinction, with a broad and powerful fan,
Puffing at all, winnows the light away;
And what hath mass or matter by itself
Lies rich in virtue and unmingled.

Agamemnon to all
TROILUS AND CRESSIDA
Act I, Scene iii, Line 26

Distinction, or competition, is a severe judge which sweeps away the less skilled or less determined, and leaves the best performers alone triumphant.

Distrust

And your large speeches may your deeds approve,
That good effects may spring from words of love.

Kent to Regan and Goneril
KING LEAR
Act I, Scene i, Line 184

And may your deeds confirm that good consequences result from expansive words spoken to show love.

Doubts

In time I may believe, yet I mistrust.
Bianca to Lucentio
TAMING OF THE SHREW
Act III, Scene i, Line 49

In the future, I may believe what you assert, but currently I am skeptical.

Our doubts are traitors
And make us lose the good we oft might win,
By fearing to attempt.
Lucio to Isabella
MEASURE FOR MEASURE
Act I, Scene iv, Line 77

Our doubts betray us by encouraging inaction, thereby making us miss opportunities.

Modest doubt is called the beacon of the wise.
Hector to Priam
TROILUS AND CRESSIDA
Act II, Scene ii, 15

Moderate doubt is known as a guide to a prudent person.

Doubts (cont'd)

Dangerous conceits are in their natures poisons,
Which at the first are scarce found to distaste,
But with a little act upon the blood
Burn like the mines of sulfur.

Iago in soliloquy
OTHELLO
Act III, Scene iii, Line 326

Subversive thoughts are like poisons, which at first seem mild to the taste, but after they work a while they cause excruciating pain.

Drama

O for a Muse of fire, that would ascend
The brightest heaven of invention,
A kingdom for a stage, princes to act,
And monarchs to behold the swelling scene!

Prologue
HENRY V
Prologue, Line 1

Oh for a goddess of the stage endowed with a fiery spirit that would achieve a heaven-like imagination and have a whole kingdom for a stage with princes as actors and kings and queens to observe the expansive scene!

𝔇rama (cont'd)

Piece out our imperfections with your thoughts:
Think, when we talk of horses, that you see them
Printing their proud hoofs i' th' receiving earth;
For 'tis your thoughts that now must deck our kings,
Carry them here and there, jumping o'er times,
Turning th' accomplishment of many years
Into an hour-glass.

Prologue
HENRY V
Prologue, Line 23

Use your imagination to fill in the gaps in the play. Imagine that when the actors speak of horses that you can see them pounding the earth with their hoofs. For you must use your mind's eye to dress our kings in fine array, move them from one location to another, and compress historical events that took years to accomplish into the short time in which they are presented on the stage.

Dreams

**O, I have passed a miserable night,
So full of fearful dreams, of ugly sights,
That, as I am a Christian faithful man,
I would not spend another such a night
Though 'twere to buy a world of happy days-
So full of dismal terror was the time!**

Clarence to Keeper
RICHARD III
Act I, Scene iv, Line 2

Oh, I have had such a terrible night of nightmares that I swear I would not agree to spend another night like it even if to do so would mean I could spend a lifetime of happy days.

Drunkenness

O thou invisible spirit of wine, if thou hast no name to be known by, let us call thee devil!

Cassio to Iago
OTHELLO
Act II, Scene iii, Line 270

Oh, you intoxicating wine, if you have no name, you should be called devil!

𝔇runkenness (cont'd)

O God! that men should put an enemy in their mouths to steal away their brains; that we should with joy, pleasure, revel, and applause transform ourselves into beasts!

Cassio to Iago
OTHELLO
Act II, Scene iii, Line 277

Oh God, that men should be so foolish to drink alcoholic beverages to make us drunk and stupid! That we should do this enthusiastically and thereby transform ourselves into beasts!

To be now a sensible man, by and by a fool, and presently a beast! O strange! Every inordinate cup is unblest, and the ingredient is a devil.

Cassio to Iago
OTHELLO
Act II, Scene iii, Line 292

To be at first a sensible man, then after some drinking, a fool; soon after, with more drinking, a beast! Every excessive cup is unblest and the wine in the cup is a devil.

Duty

**Never anything can be amiss
When simpleness and duty tender it.**
> *Theseus to all*
> *MIDSUMMER NIGHT'S DREAM*
> *Act V, Scene i, Line 82*

When honest conscientious effort is put forth, it is worthwhile, even if it is done by a simple soul.

**I am not made of stones,
But penetrable to your kind entreaties,
Albeit against my conscience and my soul.**
> *Richard to all*
> *RICHARD III*
> *Act III, Scene vii, Line 224*

I am not rigid in my hesitation, but rather I am affected by your kind requests, although I would much rather not do so.

**Since you will buckle fortune on my back,
To bear her burden, whe'er I will or no,
I must have patience to endure the load.**
> *Richard to all*
> *RICHARD III*
> *Act III, Scene vii, Line 228*

Since you will insist on my taking on this responsibility whether I say yes or no, I must have patience and do so.

Education

O this learning, what a thing it is!
Gremio to Lucentio
TAMING OF THE SHREW
Act I, Scene ii, Line 156

Education is a marvelous achievement.

Egocentricity

O, you are sick of self-love and taste with a distempered appetite. To be generous, guiltless, and of free disposition, is to take those things for bird-bolts that you deem cannon bullets.
Olivia to Malvolia
TWELFTH NIGHT
Act I, Scene v, Line 85

You are so self-centered that you look at everything in a negative way. If you were generous, guiltless, and of a free disposition, you would ignore minor barbs rather than take them to be vicious attacks.

Why, what a wasp-stung and impatient fool Art thou to break into this woman's mood, Tying thine ear to no tongue but thine own!
Northumberland to Hotspur
1 HENRY IV
Act I, Scene iii, Line 235

What a stirred-up fool you are to be babbling like a woman, listening to no one but yourself.

Egocentricity (cont'd)

**Self-love is not so vile a sin
As self-neglecting.**

Dauphin to King of France
HENRY V
Act II, Scene iv, Line 74

Although neither attitude is attractive, it is better to be guilty of self-love than it is to be guilty of self-neglect.

Enlightenment

**Full oft 'tis seen
Our means secure us, and our mere defects
Prove our commodities.**

Glouster to Old Man
KING LEAR
Act IV, Scene i, Line 19

It is often found that our capabilities make us rash while our deficiencies prove to be advantages.

Entertainment

Your tale, sir, would cure deafness.

Miranda to Prospero
THE TEMPEST
Act I, Scene ii, Line 106

Your story is so interesting that it would cure a deaf person because he or she would so want to hear it.

Ephemeral

**Let thy love be younger than thyself,
Or thy affection cannot hold the bent;
For women are as roses, whose fair flow'r
Being once displayed doth fall that very hour.**
Duke to Viola
TWELFTH NIGHT
Act II, Scene iv, Line 35

A man should choose a woman younger than himself or he will lose interest since the beauty of women is ephemeral.

Evil

No evil lost is wailed when it is gone.
Luciana to Adriana
COMEDY OF ERRORS
Act IV, Scene ii, Line 24

Everyone is pleased to see a bad situation corrected.

**The devil can cite Scripture for his purpose.
An evil soul producing holy witness
Is like a villain with a smiling cheek.**
Antonio to Bassanio
MERCHANT OF VENICE
Act I, Scene iii, Line 95

Someone doing evil deeds under the guise of piety is much like a common miscreant who smiles to disguise his nefarious actions.

Evil (cont'd)

There is some soul of goodness in things evil,
Would men observingly distill it out.
Henry V to all
HENRY V
Act IV, Scene i, Line 4

There is some small obscure measure of good that could be found in evil things if men carefully examined the situation.

All goodness
Is poison to thy stomach.
Wosley to Surrey
HENRY VIII
Act III, Scene ii, Line 282

All good thoughts, ideas, or actions are foreign to your nature.

Foul deeds will rise,
Though all the earth o'erwhelm them, to men's eyes.
Hamlet in soliloquy
HAMLET
Act I, Scene ii, Line 257

Foul deeds will become known, in spite of all efforts to conceal them.

Evil (cont'd)

**When devils will the blackest sins put on,
They do suggest at first with heavenly shows.**

Iago in soliloquy
OTHELLO
Act II, Scene iii, Line 334

When evil people intend to do very villainous deeds, they disguise their intent with very righteous appearances.

Wisdom and goodness to the vile seem vile.

Duke of Albany to Goneril
KING LEAR
Act IV, Scene ii, Line 38

A truly base person sees wisdom and goodness as very undesirable attributes.

**See thyself, devil:
Proper deformity seems not in the fiend
So horrid as in woman.**

Duke of Albany to Goneril
KING LEAR
Act IV, Scene ii, Line 59

Look at yourself, you devil: surface beauty hiding inherent ugliness doesn't appear to be so terrible in a fiend as in a woman.

Evil (cont'd)

Things bad begun make strong themselves by ill.
Macbeth to Lady Macbeth
MACBETH
Act III, Scene ii, Line 55

Activities that are started by evil actions are reinforced by more evil actions.

Excess

They are as sick that surfeit with too much as they that starve with nothing.
Nerissa to Portia
MERCHANT OF VENICE
Act I, Scene ii, Line 5

An overabundance can be as troublesome as a scarcity.

Excess (cont'd)

To gild refinèd gold, to paint the lily,
To throw a perfume on the violet,
To smooth the ice, or add another hue
Unto the rainbow, or with taper-light
To seek the beauteous eye of heaven to garnish,
Is wasteful and ridiculous excess.

Salisbury to John
KING JOHN
Act IV, Scene ii, Line 11

To plate refined gold, ... , or with a torch to try to add to the light of the sun, is wasteful and ridiculous excess.

When workmen strive to do better than well,
They do confound their skill in covetousness;
And oftentimes excusing of a fault
Doth make the fault the worse by th' excuse.

Pembroke to John
KING JOHN
Act IV, Scene ii, Line 28

When workmen try to do better than a good job, they destroy what they have done well by trying to do even better and often, by excusing a fault, make the fault look worse than it really is.

Excess (cont'd)

> **The sweetest honey**
> **Is loathsome in his own deliciousness**
> **And in the taste confounds the appetite.**
> **Therefore love moderately: long love doth so;**
> **Too swift arrives as tardy as too slow.**
>
> *Friar to Romeo*
> *ROMEO AND JULIET*
> *Act II, Scene vi, Line 11*

Excessive sweetness, if eaten in excess, overwhelms the appetite. Therefore, the sweetness of love should be enjoyed in a restrained manner.

Excitement

> **O, the blood more stirs**
> **To rouse a lion than to start a hare!**
>
> *Hotspur to Worcester*
> *1 HENRY IV*
> *Act I, Scene iii, Line 197*

Oh, it is more exciting to rouse a lion than to stir a hare.

Expectation

**Oft expectation fails, and most oft there
Where most it promises; and oft it hits
Where hope is coldest, and despair most fits.**
Helena to King
ALL'S WELL THAT ENDS WELL
Act II, Scene i, Line 142

We often find that our expectations do not work out, especially when it appears most likely they will; often our expectations do work out when we least expect them to do so.

Failure

**We fail?
But screw your courage to the sticking-place
And we'll not fail.**
Lady Macbeth to Macbeth
MACBETH
Act I, Scene vii, Line 59

We fail? Just be very courageous and we'll not fail.

Failure (cont'd)

**Th' attempt, and not the deed,
Confounds us.**

> *Lady Macbeth in soliloquy*
> *MACBETH*
> *Act II, Scene ii, Line 10*

The attempt to do the deed, rather than the actual deed, ruins us.

Faithfulness

**It grieves me
Much more for what I cannot do for you
Than what befalls myself.**

> *Antonio to Viola*
> *TWELFTH NIGHT*
> *Act III, Scene iv, Line 315*

That help which I cannot give you is more disturbing to me than that which happens to me.

Faithfulness (cont'd)

A good leg will fall, a straight back will stoop, a black beard will turn white, a curled pate will grow bald, a fair face will wither, a full eye will wax hollow. But a good heart is the sun and the moon; or, rather, the sun, and not the moon, for it shines bright and never changes, but keeps his course truly.

Henry V to Katherine
HENRY V
Act V, Scene ii, Line 157

A good leg will grow frail, a straight back will stoop, a black beard will turn white, a curled pate will grow bald, a fair face will become wrinkled, a healthy eye will become sunken. But a good heart is like the sun and the moon; or, rather, like the sun, and not the moon, for the sun shines brightly and never changes, but keeps its true course.

Be factious for redress of all these griefs, And I will set this foot of mine as far As who goes farthest.

Casca to Cassius
JULIUS CAESAR
Act I, Scene iii, Line 118

Be politically active to correct these social wrongs and I will be right in the forefront of the effort along with you.

Faithfulness (cont'd)

**The loyalty well held to fools does make
Our faith mere folly.**

Enobarbus, aside
ANTONY AND CLEOPATRA
Act III, Scene xiii, Line 42

Being steadfastly loyal to someone who becomes a fool makes that loyalty simply foolish.

Fate

**And so, from hour to hour, we ripe and ripe,
And then, from hour to hour, we rot and rot;
And thereby hangs a tale.**

Jaques quoting Touchstone to all
AS YOU LIKE IT
Act II, Scene vii, Line 26

As time goes on we first grow and mature, and then, with the further passage of time, we begin to grow old and decay, and that becomes the basis for the story of life.

𝔉𝔞𝔱𝔢 (cont'd)

**Yield not thy neck
To fortune's yoke—but let thy dauntless mind
Still ride in triumph over all mischance.**

*Lewis to Queen Margaret
3 HENRY VI
Act III, Scene iii, Line 16*

Don't give in to misfortune, but rather invent some way to overcome all bad luck.

**What fates impose, that men must needs abide;
It boots not to resist both wind and tide.**

*King Edward to all
3 HENRY VI
Act IV, Scene iii, Line 58*

What destiny imposes, men have to accept. It's useless to try to resist.

**Even so must I run on, and even so stop.
What surety of the world, what hope, what stay,
When this was now a king, and now is clay?**

*Henry to all
KING JOHN
Act V, Scene vii, Line 67*

As this king lived, so must I live, and as he died, so shall I die. What security, what hope, what support can we expect when a powerful man is doing well and then suddenly he dies.

𝔉𝔞𝔱𝔢 (cont'd)

> **O God! that one might read the book of fate,**
> **And see the revolution of the times...**
> **O, if this were seen,**
> **The happiest youth, viewing his progress through,**
> **What perils past, what crosses to ensue,**
> **Would shut the book and sit him down and die.**
>
> *King Henry to all*
> *2 HENRY IV*
> *Act III, Scene i, Lines 45,53*

Oh God! If one were to be able to see the future, the happiest young person, seeing what was coming, would sit down and die.

> **A greater power than we can contradict**
> **Hath thwarted our intents.**
>
> *Friar to Juliet*
> *ROMEO AND JULIET*
> *Act V, Scene iii, Line 153*

A greater power than we can counter has thwarted our intentions.

> **The time is out of joint. O cursèd spite**
> **That ever I was born to set it right!**
>
> *Hamlet to Horatio*
> *HAMLET*
> *Act I, Scene v, Line 188*

Things are not right. What bad luck that I have been destined to correct the problems.

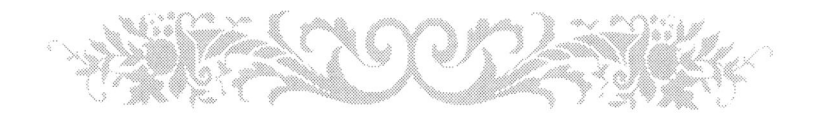

Fate (cont'd)

Our wills and fates do so contrary run
That our devices still are overthrown;
Our thoughts are ours, their ends none of our own.

King in play within play
HAMLET
Act III, Scene ii, Line 203

What we wish to do and what often happens are so different that our plans are always thwarted. We make our own plans, but the actual results are not what we intended.

Our indiscretion sometime serves us well
When our deep plots do pall, and that should learn us
There's a divinity that shapes our ends,
Rough-hew them how we will.

Hamlet to Horatio
HAMLET
Act V, Scene ii, Line 8

Our ill-considered plans sometimes give us good fortune when they fail, and we should learn by this that our lives are guided by divine forces in spite of how we try to direct them ourselves.

𝔉𝔞𝔱𝔢 (cont'd)

If it be now, 'tis not to come; if it be not to come, it will be now; if it be not now, yet it will come. The readiness is all.

> *Hamlet to Horatio*
> *HAMLET*
> *Act V, Scene ii, Line 209*

If it occurs now, it will not happen later; if it will not happen later, it will occur now; if it does not occur now, nonetheless it will happen in the future. Readiness is all that matters.

There are many events in the womb of time, which will be delivered.

> *Iago to Roderigo*
> *OTHELLO*
> *Act I, Scene iii, Line 365*

Many things will happen in the fullness of time.

As flies to wanton boys are we to the gods; They kill us for their sport.

> *Glouster to Old Man*
> *KING LEAR*
> *Act IV, Scene i, Line 36*

We get the same treatment from the gods as flies get from wanton boys. They kill us for the fun of it.

𝔉𝔞𝔱𝔢 (cont'd)

**Men must endure
Their going hence, even as their coming hither;
Ripeness is all.**

Edgar to Glouster
KING LEAR
Act V, Scene ii, Line 9

Men must endure the process of death even as they endured the process of being born. The readiness to die is the only factor.

Good wombs have borne bad sons.

Miranda to Prospero
THE TEMPEST
Act I, Scene ii, Line 120

A good woman can give birth to a son who subsequently matures into a dishonorable man.

𝔉𝔞𝔲𝔩𝔱𝔰

**His worst fault is that he is given to prayer;
he is something peevish that way; but nobody
but has his fault.**

Mistress Quickly to Simple
MERRY WIVES OF WINDSOR
Act I, Scene iv, Line 11

His worst fault is that he is always praying; he is rather foolish in that regard, but then, everyone has some fault.

Fear

Of all base passions fear is most accursed.
>Pucelle (Joan of Arc) to all
>*1 HENRY VI*
>*Act V, Scene ii, Line 18*

Of all the ignoble passions, fear is the worst.

True nobility is exempt from fear.
>*Suffolk to all*
>*2 HENRY VI*
>*Act IV, Scene i, Line 130*

Those persons who are truly noble are free of fear.

As I traveled hither through the land,
I find the people strangely fantasied;
Possessed with rumors, full of idle dreams.
Not knowing what they fear, but full of fear.
>*Bastard to John*
>*KING JOHN*
>*Act IV, Scene ii, Line 143*

As I traveled through the land to get here, I found the people full of strange notions. They are distraught with rumors, not knowing what exactly they fear, but nonetheless full of fear.

Fear (cont'd)

**To fear the foe, since fear oppresseth strength,
Gives, in your weakness, strength unto your foe.**

Carlisle to King Richard
RICHARD II
Act III, Scene ii, Line 180

It is a mistake to fear the foe since that fear diminishes your strength, thereby adding to the strength of your foe.

**Thou tremblest; and the whiteness in thy cheek
Is apter than thy tongue to tell thy errand.**

Northumberland to Morton
2 HENRY IV,
Act I, Scene i, Line 68

You tremble, and your pale face is more able than your words to explain your message.

Fear (cont'd)

**He that but fears the thing he would not know
Hath by instinct knowledge from others' eyes
That what he feared is chancèd .**

Northumberland to Morton
2 HENRY IV
Act I, Scene i, Line 85

He that is apprehensive about the thing he would rather not learn instinctively knows from someone's eyes that that which he feared has actually happened.

**I see a strange confession in thine eye.
Thou shak'st thy head, and hold'st it fear or sin
To speak a truth.**

Northumberland to Morton
2 HENRY IV
Act I, Scene i, Line 94

I see apprehension in your appearance. You're shaking your head and you believe it will be either fearful or sinful to tell what the true situation is.

**I have a faint cold fear thrills through my veins
That almost freezes up the heat of life.**

Juliet in soliloquy
ROMEO AND JULIET
Act IV, Scene iii, Line 15

I have a fear that rushes through my veins that makes me feel about to faint and chills me to the bone.

Fear (cont'd)

Fears make devils of cherubims; they never see truly.
Troilus to Cressida
TROILUS AND CRESSIDA
Act III, Scene ii, Line 64

Fear prevents realistic vision and tends to make horrors out of nothing.

Blind fear, that seeing reason leads, finds safer footing than blind reason stumbling without fear. To fear the worst oft cures the worse.
Cressida to Troilus
TROILUS AND CRESSIDA
Act III, Scene ii, Line 66

It is safer to allow fear to guide reason than to reason coldly without appropriate apprehension. Often fearing the worst prepares one to overcome the worst.

In time we hate that which we often fear.
Charmain to Cleopatra
ANTONY AND CLEOPATRA
Act I, Scene iii, Line 12

If we are often apprehensive and fearful about what someone will say or do, we will eventually dislike, or even hate, the person.

Fishing

**The pleasant'st angling is to see the fish
Cut with her golden oars the silver stream
And greedily devour the treacherous bait.**

Ursula to Hero
MUCH ADO ABOUT NOTHING
Act III, Scene i, Line 26

It is rewarding sport to watch a fish break through the surface of the water as it grasps for the bait. (Or, as is the case in the play where this line is used, it is great sport to fool someone with a false story and to watch them become convinced it is true.)

Flattery

**O that men's ears should be
To counsel deaf, but not to flattery!**

Apemantus in soliloquy
TIMON OF ATHENS
Act I, Scene ii, Line 242

It's unfortunate that men listen to people who flatter them to take advantage of them, but not listen to those that tell them the unpleasant truth without regard to other considerations.

Folly

As you have one eye upon my follies, as you hear them unfolded, turn another into the register of your own, that I may pass with a reproof the easier, sith you yourself know how easy is it to be such an offender.

Ford to Falstaff
MERRY WIVES OF WINDSOR
Act II, Scene ii, Line 169

As you view my follies from your perspective, look also at a compilation of your own, so that you will be less inclined to condemn me since you will be reminded of how easy it is to do foolish things.

**Full oft we see
Cold wisdom waiting on superfluous folly.**

Helena in soliloquy
ALL'S WELL THAT ENDS WELL
Act I, Scene i, Line 100

We often see that a wise man, or a sensible idea, is kept subordinate to a foolish man, or a bad concept.

The common curse of mankind, folly and ignorance, be thine in great revenue!

Thersites to Patroclus
TROILUS AND CRESSIDA
Act II, Scene iii, Line 25

The common curse of mankind, folly and ignorance, be yours in great abundance.

Folly (cont'd)

The amity that wisdom knits not, folly may easily untie.

Ulysses to Nestor
TROILUS AND CRESSIDA
Act II, Scene iii, Line 97

An agreement that is not made with careful evaluation may be broken easily by ill-considered action.

Though age from folly could not give me freedom, It does from childishness.

Cleopatra to Antony
ANTONY AND CLEOPATRA
Act I, Scene iii, Line 57

Although becoming a mature adult does not prevent me from being foolish sometime, nonetheless, I no longer behave childishly.

Foolishness

Lord, what fools these mortals be!

Puck to Oberon
MIDSUMMER NIGHT'S DREAM
Act III, Scene ii, Line 115

Goodness, human beings are such fools. (Spoken by Puck, a non-mortal "spirit," to Oberon, the non-mortal "King of the Fairies.")

Foolishness (cont'd)

His reasons are as two grains of wheat hid in two bushels of chaff: you shall seek all day ere you find them, and when you have them they are not worth the search.

Bassanio to Antonio
MERCHANT OF VENICE
Act I, Scene i, Line 115

He talks a great deal, but he doesn't say much of significance.

**'Tis such fools as you
That makes the world full of ill-favored children.**

Rosalind to Phebe
AS YOU LIKE IT
Act III, Scene v, Line 52

A sarcastic remark implying that a ugly person should not have children because they will also be ugly.

**There can be no kernel in this light nut;
the soul of this man is his clothes.**

Lafew to Bertram
ALL'S WELL THAT ENDS WELL
Act II, Scene v, Line 42

There is no substance to this man. Everything about him is based on appearance.

Foolishness (cont'd)

How ill white hairs become a fool and jester!
Henry V to Falstaff and all
2 HENRY IV
Act V, Scene v, Line 49

How inappropriate it is for an old person to act like a fool and jester.

Fools

Women and fools, break off your conference.
Philip to women and fools
KING JOHN
Act II, Scene i, Line 150

Women and fools, stop talking. (Not a very politically correct line in today's world, but in the play it is spoken imperiously by a king, and I include it to test the tolerance of women to a bit of mild kidding.)

Foreboding

When Fortune means to men most good,
She looks upon them with a threat'ning eye.
Pandulph to Lewis
KING JOHN
Act III, Scene iv, Line 119

Ominous prospects often turn out very well.

Forgiveness

**How much, methinks, I could despise this man
But that I am bound in charity against it!**
Wosley to Surrey
HENRY VIII
Act III, Scene ii, Line 297

How much I could hate this man, except that as a religious person I must not.

Fortune

**When Fortune means to men most good,
She looks upon them with a threat'ning eye.**
Pandulph to Lewis
KING JOHN
Act III, Scene iv, Line 119

Ominous prospects often turn out very well.

**When Fortune in her shift and change of mood
Spurns down her late beloved, all his dependents,
Which labored after him to the mountain's top
Even on their knees and hands, let him slip down,
Not one accompanying his declining foot.**
Poet to Painter
TIMON OF ATHENS
Act I, Scene i, Line 84

When capricious fortune turns on a man driving him from the heights to the depths, those who followed him when he was ascending do not remain faithful and assist him when he is descending.

Fortune (cont'd)

Well, I know not
What counts harsh fortune casts upon my face;
But in my bosom shall she never come
To make my heart her vassal.

Pompey to Caesar
ANTONY AND CLEOPATRA
Act II, Scene vi, Line 53

I don't know what misfortunes I will encounter in the future, but I will never let this woman into my affections and thus become enthralled with her.

Fortune brings in some boats that are not steered.

Pinsanio in soliloquy
CYMBELINE
Act IV, Scene iii, Line 46

Some things turn out well even though no guiding effort is expended.

Frankness

Mistake me not, I speak but as I find.

Baptista to Petruchio
TAMING OF THE SHREW
Act II, Scene i, Line 66

Do not misunderstand me–I am describing the situation as I see it.

Friendship

'Twixt such friends as we
Few words suffice.

Petruchio to Hortensio
TAMING OF THE SHREW
Act I, Scene ii, Line 63

Between friends like us few words are needed to come to an understanding.

Friendship is constant in all things
Save in the office and affairs of love.

Claudio in soliloquy
MUCH ADO ABOUT NOTHING
Act II, Scene i, Line 157

Friendship is faithful in all matters except when there is competition for the love of another.

𝔉𝔯𝔦𝔢𝔫𝔡𝔰𝔥𝔦𝔭 (cont'd)

This from a dying man receive as certain:
Where you are liberal of your loves and counsels,
Be sure you be not loose; for those you make friends
And give your hearts to, when they once perceive
The least rub in your fortunes, fall away
Like water from ye, never found again
But where they mean to sink ye.

Buckingham to all
HENRY VIII
Act II, Scene i, Line 125

Take these words from a dying man as truth: Be liberal in your dealing with people, but don't be too trusting, because even those that you treat as good friends will desert you if your good fortune slips away.

I do observe you now of late;
I have not from your eyes that gentleness
And show of love as I was wont to have.
You bear too stubborn and too strange a hand
Over your friend that loves you.

Cassius to Brutus
JULIUS CAESAR
Act I, Scene ii, Line 32

I notice that lately you are not as pleasant to me as I have been accustomed to. You are being very cold to me, even though I consider you my very good friend.

Friendship (cont'd)

**Thou dost conspire against thy friend,
If thou but think'st him wronged, and mak'st his ear
A stranger to thy thoughts.**

Othello to Iago
OTHELLO
Act III, Scene iii, Line 142

If you think your friend is being wronged and do not tell him of your suspicions, you are in effect conspiring with the wrong-doer.

**I am not of that feather to shake off
My friend when he most needs me.**

Timon to Messenger
TIMON OF ATHENS
Act I, Scene i, Line 100

I am not the kind of person who will desert my friend when he most needs my help.

Generosity

Use every man after his desert, and who shall scape whipping? Use them after your own honor and dignity. The less they deserve, the more merit in your bounty.

Hamlet to Polonius
HAMLET
Act II, Scene ii, Line 516

If you treated every man according to what he deserved, who of us would escape punishment? Rather if you treat them as you would want to be treated, even if this is better than they deserve, your generosity would be meritorious.

Gentleness

The truth you speak doth lack some gentleness.

Gonzalo to Sebastian
THE TEMPEST
Act II, Scene i, Line 133

Your truthful comments are too blunt.

Gold

> 'Tis gold
> Which buys admittance; oft it doth—yea, and 'tis gold
> Which makes the true man killed and saves the thief;
> Nay, sometime hangs both thief and true man. What
> Can it not do and undo?
>
> *Cloten in soliloquy*
> *CYMBELINE*
> *Act II, Scene iii, Line 67*

Money often gets you accepted. Money also causes the innocent men to be killed and frees the thief. Or, it can sometimes cause both to be hanged. Money can buy just about anything.

Good Fortune

> We, ignorant of ourselves,
> Beg often our own harms, which the wise pow'rs
> Deny us for our good; so find we profit
> By losing of our prayers.
>
> *Menecrates to Pompey*
> *ANTONY AND CLEOPATRA*
> *Act II, Scene i, Line 5*

We, not understanding our true nature and needs, often pray for things that would do us more harm than good. Fortunately, however, God does not satisfy our prayers, and we are better off as a consequence.

Goodness

**How far that little candle throws his beams!
So shines a good deed in a naughty world.**

Portia to Nerissa
MERCHANT OF VENICE
Act V, Scene i, Line 90

A good deed in a wicked world is like the shining of a small candle in the dark.

**There is some soul of goodness in things evil,
Would men observingly distill it out.**

Henry V to all
HENRY V
Act IV, Scene i, Line 4

There is some small obscure measure of good that could be found in evil things if men carefully examined the situation.

Greatness

Some are born great, some achieve greatness, and some have greatness thrust upon 'em.

Malvolia, reading
TWELFTH NIGHT
Act II, Scene v, Line 132

Some people are born with high social status, some people are able to achieve high social status by hard work, and some people seem to get high social status from outside forces. (In the context of the play greatness means high social position and is intended to appeal to the egocentric Malvolia, but it could just as easily apply to great accomplishments.)

Greatness (cont'd)

**Great men may jest with saints: 'tis wit in them;
But in the less, foul profanation.**

Isabella to Angelo
MEASURE FOR MEASURE
Act II, Scene ii, Line 127

A position of authority provides a man with liberties that are not tolerated in ordinary citizens.

**'Tis certain, greatness, once fall'n out with fortune,
Must fall out with men too.**

Achilles to Patroclus
TROILUS AND CRESSIDA
Act III, Scene iii, Line 76

Great men, when they encounter a series of misfortunes, will lose their status in society.

Greed

Well, whiles I am a beggar, I will rail
And say there is no sin but to be rich;
And being rich, my virtue then shall be
To say there is no vice but beggary.
Since kings break faith upon commodity,
Gain, be my lord, for I will worship thee!

Bastard in soliloquy
KING JOHN
Act II, Scene i, Line 593

As long as I'm poor, I'll complain loudly and say that it's sinful to be rich. But if I should become rich, I'll assert the opposite position. Since national leaders renege on contracts for financial advantage, I'll concentrate all my efforts on getting rich.

No man's pie is freed
From his ambitious finger.

Buckingham to Norfolk
HENRY III
Act I, Scene i, Line 52

No man's wealth is safe from his covetous activities.

Grief

O, grief hath changed me since you saw me last,
And careful hours, with Time's deformèd hand,
Have written strange defeatures in my face.
Egeon to Antipholus E.
COMEDY OF ERRORS
Act V, Scene i, Line 298

Living with grief over a long time period has aged my appearance.

Well, every one can master a grief but he that has it.
Benedict to all
MUCH ADO ABOUT NOTHING
Act III, Scene ii, Line 25

Everyone can cure a pain or an unhappiness of someone else with words of advice, but it's not so easily accomplished by the person who is afflicted.

Being that I flow in grief,
The smallest twine may lead me.
Leonato to all
MUCH ADO ABOUT NOTHING
Act IV, Scene i, Line 247

Since I am immersed in grief, any minor idea that will relieve me I am willing to try.

Grief (cont'd)

I cannot be a man with wishing; therefore I will die a woman with grieving.
Beatrice to Benedict
MUCH ADO ABOUT NOTHING
Act IV, Scene i, Line 31

To get revenge I would have to be a man, which I cannot be. Therefore I must succumb to grief.

**Give not me counsel,
Nor let no comforter delight in mine ear
But such a one whose wrongs do suit with mine.**
Leonato to Antonio
MUCH ADO ABOUT NOTHING
Act V, Scene i, Line 5

Do not try to comfort me unless you have experienced the same cause of grief that is mine.

**Men
Can counsel and speak comfort to that grief
Which they themselves not feel; but, tasting it,
Their counsel turns to passion.**
Leonato to Antonio
MUCH ADO ABOUT NOTHING
Act V, Scene i, Line 20

Men can speak comforting words to someone with a grief they themselves have not, but if they did experience it, they would themselves become emotionally distraught.

Grief (cont'd)

Moderate lamentation is the right of the dead, excessive grief the enemy to the living.

Lafew to Helena
ALL'S WELL THAT ENDS WELL
Act I, Scene i, Line 50

One should show sorrow to observe the death of a loved one and thereby honor him or her, but if grief is carried to an extreme it is damaging to the life of the person who is so grieving.

Joy absent, grief is present for that time.

Bolingbroke to Gaunt
RICHARD II
Act I, Scene iii, Line 259

If you lose some source of joy in your life, grief replaces it for the time period when it is gone.

Grief makes one hour ten.

Bolingbroke to Gaunt
RICHARD II
Act I, Scene iii, Line 261

Grief makes time seem to pass slowly.

Grief (cont'd)

Comfort's in heaven, and we are on the earth, Where nothing lives but crosses, cares, and grief.

York to the Queen
RICHARD II
Act II, Scene ii, Line 78

There is comfort in heaven, but we are on earth and we encounter nothing but thwartings, cares, and grief.

He has strangled his language in his tears.

King to all
HENRY VIII
Act V, Scene i, Line 156

He has become so emotional that he cannot speak.

Alas, poor man! grief has so wrought on him, He takes false shadows for true substances.

Marcus to himself
TITUS ANDRONICUS
Act III, Scene ii, Line 79

Alas, the man has been so wracked with grief that he sees reality in misunderstood events.

Grief (cont'd)

**Is there no pity sitting in the clouds
That sees into the bottom of my grief?**

Juliet to heaven
ROMEO AND JULIET
Act III, Scene v, Line 198

Is there not a god in heaven who can see the depth of my despair and pity me?

**Now is that noble vessel full of grief,
That it runs over even at his eyes.**

Clitus to Dardanius
JULIUS CAESAR
Act V, Scene v, Line 13

That noble man is so wracked with grief that his eyes are tearing.

Guilt

**Suspicion always haunts the guilty mind;
The thief doth fear each bush an officer.**

Richard to King Henry
3 HENRY VI
Act V, Scene vi, Line 11

The person with a guilty mind is always disturbed by suspicion. A thief fears that every bush he sees is an officer about to apprehend him.

Happiness

**Frame your mind to mirth and merriment,
Which bars a thousand harms and lengthens life.**
Messenger to Sly
TAMING OF THE SHREW
Induction, Scene ii, Line 132

Take a happy attitude towards life and you will avoid problems which in turn will result in a long life.

**With mirth and laughter let old wrinkles come,
And let my liver rather heat with wine
Than my heart cool with mortifying groans.**
Gratiano to Antonio
MERCHANT OF VENICE
Act I, Scene i, Line 80

Better to live life with a happy disposition than to encounter old age with a sour outlook.

Hate

**It better fits my blood to be disdained of all
than to fashion a carriage to rob love of any.**
John to Conrade
MUCH ADO ABOUT NOTHING
Act I, Scene iii, Line 25

I would rather be disliked by everyone than to disguise my personality to get someone to like me.

Hate (cont'd)

**Sweet love, I see, changing his property,
Turns to the sourest and most deadly hate.**
Scroop to King Richard
RICHARD II
Act III, Scene ii, Line 135

When love's distinctive quality is lost, it turns to intense hatred.

**Some devil whisper curses in my ear,
And prompt me that my tongue may utter forth
The venomous malice of my swelling heart!**
Aaron to all
TITUS ANDRONICUS
Act V, Scene iii, Line 11

Some devil whisper curses in my ear to prompt me so that I can speak the nasty hatred flowing from my angry feelings.

**See what a scourge is laid upon your hate,
That heaven finds means to kill your joys with love!**
Prince to Capulet and Montague
ROMEO AND JULIET
Act V, Scene iii, Line 292

See the disastrous consequences of the feud between your families in that heaven, or justice, has caused the death of your children as a result of their love for each other.

Historic Event

How many ages hence
Shall this our lofty scene be acted over
In states unborn and accents yet unknown!
Cassius to all
JULIUS CAESAR
Act III, Scene i, Line 111

How many ages in the future will actors re-enact this scene in countries not now existing and in languages not yet known.

Holidays

If all the year were playing holidays,
To sport would be as tedious as to work;
But when they seldom come, they wished-for come,
And nothing pleaseth but rare accidents.
Prince Hal in soliloquy
1 HENRY IV
Act I, Scene ii, Line 192

If there were only holidays, enjoying oneself would be as boring as working; but when holidays come infrequently, they are very much looked forward to because there is nothing as enjoyable as unusual events.

Honesty

Honesty coupled to beauty is to have honey a sauce to sugar.

Touchstone to Audrey
AS YOU LIKE IT
Act III, Scene iii, Line 26

A woman who is both chaste and beautiful is comparable to honey as a sauce on sugar.

To be honest, as this world goes, is to be one man picked out of ten thousand.

Hamlet to Polonius
HAMLET
Act II, Scene ii, Line 178

Very few men in the world are honorable.

Honor

Our purses shall be proud, our garments poor, For 'tis the mind that makes the body rich; And as the sun breaks through the darkest clouds So honor peereth in the meanest habit.

Petruchio to Kate
TAMING OF THE SHREW
Act IV, Scene iii, Line 168

Our attitude is more important than appearance, and if we are honorable, this will be seen in spite of tawdry clothing.

Honor (cont'd)

> **Honors thrive**
> **When rather from our acts we them derive**
> **Than our fore-goers.**
>
> *King to Bertram*
> *ALL'S WELL THAT ENDS WELL*
> *Act II, Scene iii, Line 134*

More honor is achieved by our actions than on the basis of who our ancestors are.

> **If it be aught toward the general good,**
> **Set honor in one eye and death i' the other**
> **And I will look on both indifferently.**
> **For let the gods so speed me as I love**
> **The name of honor more than I fear death.**
>
> *Brutus to Cassius*
> *JULIUS CAESAR*
> *Act I, Scene ii, Line 85*

If the proposition for action is directed toward the well being of the society, whether it will result in honor or death for me is immaterial. I hope to prosper because I am more interested in acting in an honorable manner than I am concerned about avoiding death.

> **Life every man holds dear; but the dear man**
> **Holds honor far more precious-dear than life.**
>
> *Hector to all*
> *TROILUS AND CRESSIDA*
> *Act V, Scene iii, Line 27*

Every man holds life to be precious, but the man of quality holds honor to be more important even than his own life.

Honor (cont'd)

If you were born to honor, show it now;
If put upon you, make the judgment good
That thought you worthy of it.

Marina to Lysimachus
PERICLES
Act IV, Scene vi, Line 85

If you were born to a high position, demonstrate that you are worthy of the status. If you were chosen by others to assume a high position, prove by your actions that they made a valid judgment.

Hope

Oft expectation fails, and most oft there
Where most it promises; and oft it hits
Where hope is coldest, and despair most fits.

Helena to King
ALL'S WELL THAT ENDS WELL
Act II, Scene i, Line 142

We often find that our expectations do not work out, especially when it appears most likely they will; often our expectations do work out when we least expect them to do so.

The miserable have no other medicine
But only hope.

Claudio to Duke
MEASURE FOR MEASURE
Act III, Scene i, Line 2

Those who are miserable have only hope as a means of relief.

Hope (cont'd)

Hope to joy is little less in joy
Than hope enjoyed.

Northumberland to Bolingbroke
RICHARD II
Act II, Scene iii, Line 15

Anticipation of a happy event gives one almost as much happiness as the event itself.

I do spy a kind of hope,
Which craves as desperate an execution
As that is desperate which we would prevent.

Friar to Juliet
ROMEO AND JULIET
Act IV, Scene i, Line 68

I see a possible plan of action that requires a very desperate operation, which is comparable in danger to the desperate problem that is to be corrected.

The ample proposition that hope makes
In all designs begun on earth below
Fails in the promised largeness. Checks and disasters
Grow in the veins of actions highest reared.

Agamemnon to all
TROILUS AND CRESSIDA
Act I, Scene iii, Line 3

The great good hoped for from programs engaged in by humans does not occur as expected because problems are inherent in even the most exalted of human efforts.

Hope (cont'd)

Death may usurp on nature many hours,
And yet the fire of life kindle again
The o'erpressed spirits.
Cerimon to all
PERICLES
Act III, Scene ii, Line 81

A deathlike coma may take much time from living, but recovery may still be achieved.

Hospitality

Unbidden guests
Are often welcomest when they are gone.
Bedford to Talbot
1 HENRY VI
Act II, Scene ii, Line 55

It's often a welcome relief when uninvited guests leave.

Humility

Truly, sir, the better for my foes and the worse for my friends.
Marry, sir, my friends praise me and make an ass of me. Now my foes tell me plainly I am an ass; so that by my foes, sir, I profit in the knowledge of myself, and by my friends I am abused.

Clown to Duke
TWELFTH NIGHT
Act V, Scene i, Line 10

Truly, sir, I am better off because of my enemies and worse off because of my friends. This is because my friends praise me and ignore my bad characteristics while my enemies bluntly tell me of my faults. Thus my foes cause me to profit from a true knowledge of myself, whereas my friends do me harm by not encouraging me to reform.

Hypocrisy

Shame to him whose cruel striking
Kills for faults of his own liking!

Duke in soliloquy
MEASURE FOR MEASURE
Act III, Scene ii, Line 250

Shame to the person who condemns another for a misdeed for which he himself is guilty.

Hypocrisy (cont'd)

**Well, whiles I am a beggar, I will rail
And say there is no sin but to be rich;
And being rich, my virtue then shall be
To say there is no vice but beggary.
Since kings break faith upon commodity,
Gain, be my lord, for I will worship thee!**

Bastard in soliloquy
KING JOHN
Act II, Scene i, Line 593

As long as I'm poor, I'll complain loudly and say that it's sinful to be rich. But if I should become rich, I'll assert the opposite position. Since national leaders renege on contracts for financial advantage, I'll concentrate all my efforts on getting rich.

Idleness

**Ten thousand harms, more than the ills I know,
My idleness doth hatch.**

Antony in soliloquy
ANTONY AND CLEOPATRA
Act I, Scene ii, Line 125

Because of my trivial activities, I am not taking care of important matters which is going to result in many penalties.

Ignorance

The common curse of mankind, folly and ignorance, be thine in great revenue!

Thersites to Patroclus
TROILUS AND CRESSIDA
Act II, Scene iii, Line 25

The common curse of mankind, folly and ignorance, be yours in great abundance.

Illegitimacy

**Why bastard? wherefore base?
When my dimensions are as well compact,
My mind as generous, and my shape as true,
As honest madam's issue?**

Edmund in soliloquy
KING LEAR
Act I, Scene ii, Line 6

Why are bastards considered base? Is not my body of good appearance and am I not as intelligent as the offspring of faithful wives?

Illness

> We are not ourselves
> When nature, being oppressed, commands the mind
> To suffer with the body.
>
> *Lear to Glouster*
> *KING LEAR*
> *Act II, Scene iv, Line 102*

We can't think clearly when we are sick, because the mind suffers along with the body.

Imagination

> The poet's eye, in a fine frenzy rolling,
> Doth glance from heaven to earth, from earth to heaven;
> And as imagination bodies forth
> The forms of things unknown, the poet's pen
> Turns them to shapes, and gives to airy nothing
> A local habitation and a name.
>
> *Theseus to all*
> *MIDSUMMER NIGHT'S DREAM*
> *Act V, Scene i, Line 12*

The writer's imagination enables him to use his "pen" to transform thoughts to "reality" on paper by formulating them into a context with names and places.

Immoderation

**As surfeit is the father of much fast,
So every scope by the immoderate use
Turns to restraint.**

Claudio to Lucio
MEASURE FOR MEASURE
Act I, Scene ii, Line 122

Excess eating is the cause of much fasting. Similarly, if every liberty is exploited, it will result in incurring restraint.

Impatience

My business cannot brook this dalliance.

Merchant to Antipholus E.
COMEDY OF ERRORS
Act IV, Scene i, Line 59

My activities cannot tolerate your stalling.

This weighty business will not brook delay.

Cardinal to Buckingham
2 HENRY VI
Act I, Scene i, Line 168

This important business will not allow delay.

Imperatives

Strong reasons makes strange actions.
Lewis to Pandulph
KING JOHN
Act III, Scene iv, Line 182

Important reasons justify unusual actions.

Impertinence

**What's that to thee? Why may I not demand
Of thine affairs as well as thou of mine?**
Hubert to Bastard
KING JOHN
Act V, Scene vi, Line 4

I have just as much right to demand to know what you're doing as you have to demand an explanation from me regarding my actions.

Importance

**I have important business,
The tide whereof is now.**
Diomedes to Achilles
TROILUS AND CRESSIDA
Act V, Scene i, Line 81

I have important business which must be taken care of now.

Imprudence

Why strew'st thou sugar on that bottled spider
Whose deadly web ensnareth thee about?
Fool, fool! thou whet'st a knife to kill thyself.
Margaret to Elizabeth
RICHARD III
Act I, Scene iii, Line 241

Why are you pleasant to that vicious person who will cause your downfall? Fool, you sharpen the knife that will kill you.

The man that once did sell the lion's skin
While the beast lived, was killed with hunting him.
Henry V to Montjoy
HENRY V
Act IV, Scene iii, Line 93

Shakespeare's more elegant way of saying "Don't count your chickens before they're hatched."

We may outrun
By violent swiftness that which we run at,
And lose by over-running.
Norfolk to Buckingham
HENRY VIII
Act I, Scene i, Line 141

If we attack someone or some political problem too vigorously the situation may get out of control and result in our losing our objective.

Infidelity

> O curse of marriage,
> That we can call these delicate creatures ours,
> And not their appetites! I had rather be a toad
> And live upon the vapor of a dungeon
> Than keep a corner in the thing I love
> For other's uses.
>
> *Othello in soliloquy*
> *OTHELLO*
> *Act III, Scene iii, Line 268*

Oh, the curse of marriage is that we can say that our beautiful wives are ours, but not that they keep their sexual interest only for us. I would rather be a loathsome creature living in a detestable place than live with the knowledge that my wife is unfaithful.

Ingratitude

> I hate ingratitude more in a man
> Than lying, vainness, babbling drunkenness,
> Or any taint of vice whose strong corruption
> Inhabits our frail blood.
>
> *Viola to Antonio*
> *TWELFTH NIGHT*
> *Act III, Scene iv, Line 335*

I hate ingratitude more than lying, vainness, noisy drunkenness, or any kind of vice that a man might harbor.

Ingratitude (cont'd)

**One good deed dying tongueless
Slaughters a thousand waiting upon that.
Our praises are our wages.**

Hermione to Leontes
WINTER'S TALE
Act I, Scene ii, Line 92

If a good deed is not praised, that lack of praise discourages many other good deeds that otherwise would follow. Praise for our good deeds is our reward.

Injustice

Some rise by sin, and some by virtue fall.

Escalus to Angelo
MEASURE FOR MEASURE
Act II, Scene i, Line 38

Some people improve their status by improper means, while some who perform virtuous deeds lose status.

**More pity that the eagles should be mewed,
Whiles kites and buzzards prey at liberty.**

Hastings to Richard
RICHARD III
Act I, Scene i, Line 132

It is a shame that great men should be restrained while much lesser men do as they wish.

Injustice (cont'd)

**The world is grown so bad
That wrens make prey where eagles dare not perch.**

Richard to Elizabeth
RICHARD III
Act I, Scene iii, Line 69

It is a shame that great men should be restrained while much lesser men do as they wish.

**In the corrupted currents of this world
Offense's gilded hand may shove by justice,
And oft 'tis seen the wicked prize itself
Buys out the law.**

Claudius in soliloquy
HAMLET
Act III, Scene iii, Line 57

In this deceitful world money in the hand of the offender may thwart justice, and often it happens that the money obtained from unlawful acts is used to buy freedom from prosecution.

Injustice (cont'd)

Through tattered clothes small vices do appear;
Robes and furred gowns hide all. Plate sin with gold,
And the strong lance of justice hurtless breaks;
Arm it in rags, a pygmy's straw does pierce it.

Lear to Glouster
KING LEAR
Act IV, Scene vi, Line 161

Minor offenses are readily noted in poor people whereas wealth can disguise misdeeds. Wealthy lawbreakers cannot be brought to justice, but poor people are easily prosecuted.

'Tis gold
Which buys admittance; oft it doth—yea, and 'tis gold
Which makes the true man killed and saves the thief;
Nay, sometime hangs both thief and true man. What
Can it not do and undo?

Cloten in soliloquy
CYMBELINE
Act II, Scene iii, Line 67

Money often gets you accepted. Money also causes the innocent men to be killed and frees the thief. Or, it can sometimes cause both to be hanged. Money can buy just about anything.

Insanity

Madness in great ones must not unwatched go.
Claudius to Polonius
HAMLET
Act III, Scene i, Line 188

The insanity of important public figures must not be ignored.

Canst thou not minister to a mind diseased,
Pluck from the memory a rooted sorrow,
Raze out the written troubles of the brain,
And with some sweet oblivious antidote
Cleanse the stuffed bosom of that perilous stuff
Which weighs upon the heart?
Macbeth to Doctor
MACBETH
Act V, Scene iii, Line 40

Can't you treat a mentally ill person by removing from the memory some old sorrow and other troubles with some medicine that will clean the stuffed-up bosom which disturbs the innermost thoughts?

Insecurity

There is no sure foundation set on blood,
No certain life achieved by others' death.
John in soliloquy
KING JOHN
Act IV, Scene ii, Line 104

Killing others is not a sure way to improve your own position.

Insecurity (cont'd)

**Even so must I run on, and even so stop.
What surety of the world, what hope, what stay,
When this was now a king, and now is clay?**

Henry to all
KING JOHN
Act V, Scene vii, Line 67

As this king lived, so must I live, and as he died, so shall I die. What security, what support, can we expect when a powerful man is doing well and then suddenly he dies?

Jealousy

**The venom clamors of a jealous woman
Poisons more deadly than a mad dog's tooth.**

Abbess to Adriana
COMEDY OF ERRORS
Act V, Scene i, Line 69

The vicious complaints of a jealous woman destroy a relationship.

**O, beware of jealousy!
It is the green-eyed monster, which doth mock
The meat it feeds on.**

Iago to Othello
OTHELLO
Act III, Scene iii, Line 165

Beware of becoming jealous. It will consume you and then torture you as it does so.

Jealousy (cont'd)

I'll see before I doubt; when I doubt, prove;
And on the proof there is no more but this—
Away at once with love or jealousy!

Othello to Iago
OTHELLO
Act III, Scene iii, Line 190

Before I doubt the faithfulness of my wife I will have to see some evidence. Then I will prove the case one way or the other. If she is unfaithful I will reject her. If she is faithful I will reject jealousy.

I never gave him cause.

But jealous souls will not be answered so;
They are not ever jealous for the cause,
But jealous for they're jealous. 'Tis a monster
Begot upon itself, born on itself.

Desdemona to Emelia and response
OTHELLO
Act III, Scene iv, Line 159

Jealous people don't accept assurances. Truth is irrelevant. Jealousy is self-engendered.

Joy

How much better is it to weep at joy than to joy at weeping!

Leonato to all
MUCH ADO ABOUT NOTHING
Act I, Scene i, Line 25

It is better to weep thankfully at someone's happiness than it is to be happy at someone's unhappiness.

Silence is the perfectest herald of joy.

Claudio to Beatrice
MUCH ADO ABOUT NOTHING
Act II, Scene i, Line 274

Intense joy causes speechlessness.

Things won are done; joy's soul lies in the doing.

Cressida in soliloquy
TROILUS AND CRESSIDA
Act I, Scene ii, Line 273

Any objective that is achieved loses its appeal. True pleasure comes from working toward the objective.

Joy (cont'd)

**It gives me wonder great as my content
To see you here before me. O my soul's joy!
If after every tempest come such calms,
May the winds blow till they have wakened death!**
Othello to Desdemona
OTHELLO
Act II, Scene i, Line 181

I am as surprised as I am pleased that you got here before me. If after every storm the great pleasure of this moment would occur, I welcome even more severe storms.

Judgment

**To offend and judge are distinct offices,
And of opposèd natures.**
Portia to Arragon
MERCHANT OF VENICE
Act II, Scene ix, Line 60

Those that commit an offense must not be their own judges, since they have a conflict of interest.

Forbear to judge, for we are sinners all.
King to Warwick
2 HENRY VI
Act III, Scene iii, Line 31

"Judge not that you be not judged."

Judgment (cont'd)

> **Blest are those**
> **Whose blood and judgment are so well commeddled**
> **That they are not a pipe for Fortune's finger**
> **To sound what stop she please.**
>
> *Hamlet to Horatio*
> *HAMLET*
> *Act III, Scene ii, Line 65*

They are blest who have a good balance between passion and judgment so that they, rather than chance, determine the direction of their lives.

> **I see men's judgments are**
> **A parcel of their fortunes, and things outward**
> **Do draw the inward quality after them**
> **To suffer all alike.**
>
> *Enobarbus, aside*
> *ANTONY AND CLEOPATRA*
> *Act III, Scene xiii, Line 31*

I see that men's judgments are affected by their misfortune, and these misfortunes cause the deterioration of their character.

Justice

**Thieves for their robbery have authority
When judges steal themselves.**
> *Angelo in soliloquy*
> MEASURE FOR MEASURE
> *Act II, Scene ii, Line 176*

Illegal acts by the citizenry are encouraged when law enforcement authorities break the law.

**Do not count it holy
To hurt by being just.**
> *Andromache to Hector*
> TROILUS AND CRESSIDA
> *Act V, Scene iii, Line 19*

Do not believe you are acting in a sacred manner if your application of justice is hurtful to someone.

Law

**We must not make a scarecrow of the law,
Setting it up to fear the birds of prey,
And let it keep one shape till custom make it
Their perch, and not their terror.**
> *Angelo to Escalus*
> MEASURE FOR MEASURE
> *Act II, Scene i, Line 1*

We must not make the law a facade intended to deter offenders, but not actually punishing them; for then people will manipulate the law for their own use rather than fear its penalties.

Lethargy

I were better to be eaten to death with a rust than to be scoured to nothing with perpetual motion.

Falstaff to Chief Justice
2 HENRY IV
Act I, Scene ii, Line 206

It's better to die from drinking too much than to become emaciated from too much exercise. (The quick-witted rationalization of an over-indulgent lazy man, which describes Falstaff, the speaker.)

Life

All the world's a stage,
And all the men and women merely players;
They have their exits and entrances,
And one man in his time plays many parts.

Jaques to all
AS YOU LIKE IT
Act II, Scene vii, Line 139

The world is like a stage and people are like actors. They come and they go, and any given man does many things in his lifetime. (Shakespeare borrows this stock metaphor from classical literature but sets it down in poetry. Then he uses the line in the play to introduce a famous speech by Jaques describing the "Seven Ages of Man.")

Life (cont'd)

The web of our life is of a mingled yarn, good and ill together.

Second Lord to first Lord
ALL'S WELL THAT ENDS WELL
Act IV, Scene iii, Line 66

No one is all good or all bad; we are all a mixture of virtues and faults.

I am so out of love with life that I will sue to be rid of it.

Claudio to Duke
MEASURE FOR MEASURE
Act III, Scene i, Line 170

I am so unhappy with my life that I am ready to die. (This is a not uncommon statement made in today's world by men on "Death Row," which is the situation of the speaker of this line in Shakespeare's "Measure for Measure.")

Out, out, brief candle!
Life's but a walking shadow, a poor player
That struts and frets his hour upon the stage
And then is heard no more.

Macbeth to Seyton
MACBETH
Act V, Scene v, Line 23

End, brief life. Life's nothing but an intangible essence that appears on earth for a short time and then is no longer heard from.

Life (cont'd)

> **We are such stuff**
> **As dreams are made on, and our little life**
> **Is rounded with a sleep.**
>
> *Prospero to Ferdinand*
> *THE TEMPEST*
> *Act IV, Scene i, Line 156*

We humans are as ephemeral as dreams and our short life on earth is preceded by nothing and is followed by nothing.

Limitations

> **There's nothing situate under heaven's eye**
> **But hath his bound, in earth, in sea, in sky.**
>
> *Luciana to Adrian*
> *COMEDY OF ERRORS*
> *Act II, Scene i, Line 16*

Everything on earth has restraints which are determined by its peculiar characteristics.

> **If to do were as easy as to know what to do, chapels**
> **had been churches, and poor men's cottages**
> **prince's palaces.**
>
> *Portia to Nerissa*
> *MERCHANT OF VENICE*
> *Act I, Scene ii, Line 12*

It is much easier to know what to do than to actually accomplish it.

Love

> **I saw her coral lips to move,**
> **And with her breath she did perfume the air.**
> **Sacred and sweet was all I saw in her**
>
> Lucentio to Tranio
> TAMING OF THE SHREW
> Act I, Scene i, Line 171

I saw her lips speak and her breath was very sweet. I only saw her to be sacred and sweet. (Coral lips and perfumed breath were common expressions of female beauty used in sonnets, as, for example, Shakespeare lampoons in his sonnet number 130.)

> **Kindness in women, not their beauteous looks,**
> **Shall win my love.**
>
> Hortensio to Tranio
> TAMING OF THE SHREW
> Act IV, Scene ii, Line 41

From now on I'm going to love women who are kind, and I'm not going to be looking for beauty. (This is one of the few places in Shakespeare's plays where men give beauty a lower rating than other virtues when it comes to women.)

> **As in the sweetest bud**
> **The eating canker dwells, so eating love**
> **inhabits in the finest wits of all.**
>
> Proteus to Valentine
> TWO GENTLEMEN OF VERONA
> Act I, Scene i, Line 42

Just as a flower bud may be eaten by a destructive grub, so love damages even the wisest people.

Love (cont'd)

**O, how this spring of love resembleth
The uncertain glory of an April day,
Which now shows all the beauty of the sun,
And by and by a cloud takes all away!**

Proteus in soliloquy
TWO GENTLEMEN OF VERONA
Act I, Scene iii, Line 84

The beginnings of love are beset by ups and downs.

**Ay me! For all that I could ever read,
Could ever hear by tale or history,
The course of true love never did run smooth.**

Lysander to Hermia
MIDSUMMER NIGHT'S DREAM
Act I, Scene i, Line 132

It is widely observed that true love encounters many obstacles.

**Things base and vile, holding no quantity,
Love can transpose to form and dignity.**

Helena in soliloquy
MIDSUMMER NIGHT'S DREAM
Act I, Scene i, Line 232

Things or persons that are ugly can be transformed to appear beautiful in the eyes of the beholder who is in love.

𝕷𝖔𝖛𝖊 (cont'd)

**Love's feeling is more soft and sensible
Than are the tender horns of cockled snails.**

*Berowne to all
LOVE'S LABOR'S LOST
Act IV, Scene iii, Line 332*

The feelings of love are very tender, softer even than the antennae of snails.

**When love speaks, the voice of all the gods
Make heaven drowsy with the harmony.**

*Berowne to all
LOVE'S LABOR'S LOST
Act IV, Scene iii, Line 339*

When someone speaks of his or her love, it is so sweet that the gods echo it harmoniously and make heaven drowsy.

**Love is blind, and lovers cannot see
The pretty follies that themselves commit.**

*Jessica to Lorenzo
MERCHANT OF VENICE
Act II, Scene vi, Line 36*

Love clouds the reason and those in love don't realize the foolish things they do.

Love (cont'd)

**O love, be moderate, allay thy ecstasy,
In measure rain thy joy, scant this excess!
I feel too much thy blessing.**

Portia, aside
MERCHANT OF VENICE
Act III, Scene ii, Line 111

Oh, I must restrain this overwhelming enthusiasm for love. My emotions are too much for me to bear.

**If thou rememb'rest not the slightest folly
That ever love did make thee run into,
Thou hast not loved.**

Silvius to Corin
AS YOU LIKE IT
Act II, Scene iv, Line 31

If you cannot remember the most inconsequential foolishness that being in love made you do, you have not truly loved.

We that are true lovers run into strange capers; but as all is mortal in nature, so is all nature in love mortal in folly.

Touchstone to Rosalind
AS YOU LIKE IT
Act II, Scene iv, Line 49

True lovers do strange things, but this is because as all life is mortal, by their foolishness lovers show themselves to be part of nature and therefore mortal.

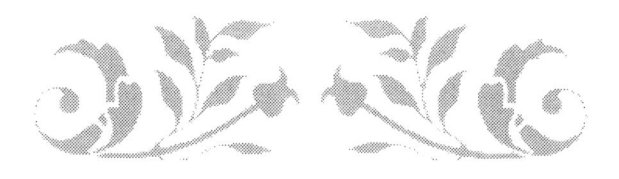

Love (cont'd)

Love is merely a madness, and, I tell you, deserves as well a dark house and a whip as madmen do.

Rosalind to Orlando
AS YOU LIKE IT
Act III, Scene ii, Line 376

Confinement in a dark room and whipping were the "shock" treatments used by Elizabethans to cure the insane, and the same treatment is suggested to cure the insanity of love.

Who ever loved that loved not at first sight?

Phebe to herself, quoting C. Marlowe
AS YOU LIKE IT
Act III, Scene v, Line 81

Is there anyone who has ever loved that didn't love at first sight? (This is a line from C. Marlowe, who is referred to in the line previous to this one as a dead shepherd since he recently had been killed in a bar-room fight.)

So holy and so perfect is my love, And I in such a poverty of grace, That I shall think it a most plenteous crop To glean the broken ears after the man That the main harvest reaps. Loose now and then A scatt'red smile, and that I'll live upon.

Silvius to Phebe
AS YOU LIKE IT
Act III, Scene v, Line 98

My love for you is so complete that even though you do not love me I will dote on you and defer to the person you love with the hope that you will give me an occasional smile to sustain me.

Love (cont'd)

Men have died from time to time, and worms have eaten them, but not for love.
> *Rosalind to Orlando*
> *AS YOU LIKE IT*
> *Act IV, Scene i, Line 96*

Men have died in the past, but they didn't die for love.

I had rather hear my dog bark at a crow than a man swear that he loves me.
> *Beatrice to Benedict*
> *MUCH ADO ABOUT NOTHING*
> *Act I, Scene i, Line 116*

I'd rather listen to something unpleasant than to listen to a man swearing that he loves me.

**In her bosom I'll unclasp my heart
And take her hearing prisoner with the force
And strong encounter of my amorous tale.**
> *Don Pedro to Claudio*
> *MUCH ADO ABOUT NOTHING*
> *Act I, Scene i, Line 291*

I will privately tell her of my love so emphatically that she will listen intently.

Love (cont'd)

**Friendship is constant in all things
Save in the office and affairs of love.**

Claudio in soliloquy
MUCH ADO ABOUT NOTHING
Act II, Scene i, Line 157

Friendship is faithful in all matters except when there is competition for the love of another.

If music be the food of love, play on.

Duke to All
TWELFTH NIGHT
Act I, Scene i, Line 1

If music enhances love, continue to play.

**What is love? 'Tis not hereafter;
Present mirth hath present laughter;
What's to come is still unsure.
In delay there lies no plenty,
Then come kiss me, sweet and twenty;
Youth's a stuff will not endure.**

Clown to Toby and Andrew
TWELFTH NIGHT
Act II, Scene iii, Line 44

Love is a present pleasure, and since the future is uncertain, enjoy youth and love before it expires.

Love (cont'd)

**Let thy love be younger than thyself,
Or thy affection cannot hold the bent;
For women are as roses, whose fair flow'r
Being once displayed doth fall that very hour.**

Duke to Viola
TWELFTH NIGHT
Act II, Scene iv, Line 35

A man should choose a woman younger than himself or he will lose interest since the beauty of women is ephemeral.

**There is no woman's sides
Can bide the beating of so strong a passion
As love doth give my heart.**

Duke to Viola
TWELFTH NIGHT
Act II, Scene iv, Line 92

As a man, I know that no woman has the strength to love as passionately as I do.

**We men may say more, swear more, but indeed
Our shows are more than will; for still we prove
Much in our vows, but little in our love.**

Viola to Duke
TWELFTH NIGHT
Act II, Scene iv, Line 115

We men profess our love more than agrees with our true passion; we always prove to be more bombastic than faithful.

Love (cont'd)

Love sought is good, but given unsought is better.
Olivia to Viola
TWELFTH NIGHT
Act III, Scene i, Line 153

Love is more pleasant if one does not have to convince someone to love you.

I have said too much unto a heart of stone,
And laid mine honor too unchary on't.
There's something in me that reproves my fault;
But such a headstrong potent fault it is
That it but mocks reproof.
Olivia to Viola
TWELFTH NIGHT
Act III, Scene iv, Line 187

I have professed too much love to a disdaining person and put my self-respect incautiously on the stone that is his or her heart. I know somewhere deep inside me that what I'm doing is wrong, but I am so helplessly in love that I'm ignoring my inner voice.

O powerful love, that in some respects makes a beast a man; in some other a man a beast.
Falstaff in soliloquy
MERRY WIVES OF WINDSOR
Act V, Scene iv, Line 4

Love is a very potent emotion. It has the power to change a man from a crude antagonistic boor into a well-mannered lover in hope of appealing to a loved one, or love can change a reasonable man into a lustful brute in pursuit of sex.

Love (cont'd)

> **'Twere all one
> That I should love a bright particular star
> And think to wed it, he is so above me.
> In his bright radiance and collateral light
> Must I be comforted, not in his sphere.**
>
> *Helena in soliloquy*
> *ALL'S WELL THAT ENDS WELL*
> *Act I, Scene i, Line 81*

It's unfortunate that I should be in love with and hope to marry a man who is far superior to me in social position. I must be happy just having some association with him and not expect to marry him.

> **The hind that would be mated by the lion
> Must die for love.**
>
> *Helena in soliloquy*
> *ALL'S WELL THAT ENDS WELL*
> *Act I, Scene i, Line 87*

The deer that is attracted to the lion will find it is a fatal attraction. (This is an analogy to a human situation where the hind represents a woman with a low social status and the lion represents a man with a high social status.)

Love (cont'd)

**If I depart from thee, I cannot live;
And in thy sight to die, what were it else
But like a pleasant slumber in thy lap?**

Suffolk to Queen
2 HENRY VI
Act III, Scene ii, Line 388

If I have to leave you, life will be like death, but if I were to die while with you it would merely be like a pleasant nap.

**Love is a smoke raised with the fume of sighs;
Being purged, a fire sparkling in lovers' eyes;
Being vexed, a sea nourished with lovers' tears.
What is it else? A madness most discreet,
A choking gall, and a preserving sweet.**

Romeo to Benvolio
ROMEO AND JULIET
Act I, Scene i, Line 188

Love is like a disturbed vision disguised by smoke generated by the longing sighs of one in love; when cleared (that is, requited) it's seen by the sparkle in lover's eyes; when distraught, love is like a sea fed with lover's tears. It's also a kind of insanity, or an incapacitating annoyance, or a heart-warming pleasure.

Love (cont'd)

**I cannot bound a pitch above dull woe.
Under love's heavy burthen do I sink.**

*Romeo to Mercutio
ROMEO AND JULIET
Act I, Scene iv, Line 21*

I cannot raise myself above a boring misery because I am weighted down by unrequited love.

**Is love a tender thing? It is too rough,
Too rude, too boist'rous, and it pricks like thorn.**

*Romeo to Mercutio
ROMEO AND JULIET
Act I, Scene iv, Line 25*

Is love a tender experience? No, it's rough, rude, boisterous, and it hurts like the sting of a thorn.

**My only love, sprung from my only hate!
Too early seen unknown, and known too late!
Prodigious birth of love it is to me
That I must love a loathèd enemy.**

*Juliet to Nurse
ROMEO AND JULIET
Act I, Scene v, Line 138*

My first and only love is the offspring of the only family I hate. I saw him before I knew the connection, and then it was too late. It's a monstrous birth of love when he whom I love is really a member of a hated family.

Love (cont'd)

If thou dost love, pronounce it faithfully.

> *Juliet to Romeo*
> *ROMEO AND JULIET*
> *Act II, Scene ii, Line 94*

If you say you love me, tell me so truthfully.

My bounty is as boundless as the sea,
My love as deep; the more I give to thee,
The more I have, for both are infinite.

> *Juliet to Romeo*
> *ROMEO AND JULIET*
> *Act II, Scene ii, Line 133*

My capacity to give love is as limitless as the ocean and the depth of my love is a deep as the ocean. Moreover, the more love I give to you the more I have, for both are infinite.

How silver-sweet sound lovers' tongues by night,
Like softest music to attending ears!

> *Romeo to Juliet*
> *ROMEO AND JULIET*
> *Act II, Scene ii, Line 166*

How pleasant sounding are lovers' words in the evening, like very soft music to carefully listening ears.

Love (cont'd)

        Young men's love then lies
Not truly in their hearts, but in their eyes.
> *Friar to Romeo*
> *ROMEO AND JULIET*
> *Act II, Scene iii, Line 67*

Young men are fickle and become infatuated easily on the basis of appearance.

        Love's heralds should be thoughts,
Which ten times faster glide than the sun's beams
Driving back shadows over low'ring hills.
> *Juliet in soliloquy*
> *ROMEO AND JULIET*
> *Act II, Scene v, Line 4*

Messengers between lovers should speed as quickly as thoughts, which are much faster than the sun's beams driving away shadows.

        The sweetest honey
Is loathsome in his own deliciousness
And in the taste confounds the appetite.
Therefore love moderately: long love doth so;
Too swift arrives as tardy as too slow.
> *Friar to Romeo*
> *ROMEO AND JULIET*
> *Act II, Scene vi, Line 11*

Excessive sweetness, if eaten in excess, overwhelms the appetite. Therefore, the sweetness of love should be enjoyed in a restrained manner.

Love (cont'd)

> **They say all lovers swear more performance
> than they are able.**
>
> *Cressida to Troilus*
> *TROILUS AND CRESSIDA*
> *Act III, Scene ii, Line 78*

It is said that all lovers promise to love more and to do more than they prove to be capable of.

> **Time, force, and death,**
> **Do to this body what extremes you can,**
> **But the strong base and building of my love**
> **Is as the very center of the earth,**
> **Drawing all things to it.**
>
> *Cressida to Pandarus*
> *TROILUS AND CRESSIDA*
> *Act IV, Scene ii, Line 100*

Let the forces of nature do to my body what terrible things they can; nonetheless, the love that is the foundation of my life is at the core of my being.

> **She loved me for the dangers I had passed,**
> **And I loved her that she did pity them.**
>
> *Othello to Duke and all*
> *OTHELLO*
> *Act I, Scene iii, Line 167*

She loved me because of all the dangers I had overcome, and I loved her because she had such concern for me.

Love (cont'd)

**It gives me wonder great as my content
To see you here before me. O my soul's joy!
If after every tempest come such calms,
May the winds blow till they have wakened death!**

Othello to Desdemona
OTHELLO
Act II, Scene i, Line 181

I am as surprised as I am pleased that you got here before me.
If after every storm the great pleasure of this moment
would occur, I would welcome even more severe storms.

**I'll see before I doubt; when I doubt, prove;
And on the proof there is no more but this–
Away at once with love or jealousy!**

Othello to Iago
OTHELLO
Act III, Scene iii, Line 190

Before I doubt the faithfulness of my wife I will have to see
some evidence. Then I will prove the case one way or the
other. If she is unfaithful I will reject her. If she is faithful
I will reject jealousy.

Love (cont'd)

**Speak of me as I am. Nothing extenuate,
Nor set down aught in malice. Then must you speak
Of one that loved not wisely, but too well.**
Othello to all
OTHELLO
Act V, Scene ii, Line 342

When you describe these unfortunate events do not
make excuses for me, nor speak with malice toward me.
Simply say that I loved too intensely, but not very wisely.

**Love's not love
When it is mingled with regards that stands
Aloof from th' entire point.**
France to Burgundy
KING LEAR
Act I, Scene i, Line 238

Love's not true love when it's involved with irrelevant
considerations.

If it be love indeed, tell me how much.

There's beggary in the love that can be reckoned.
Cleopatra to Antony and response
ANTONY AND CLEOPATRA
Ace I, Scene i, Line 14

Love is impoverished if a quantity can be assigned to it.

Love (cont'd)

**Now for the love of Love and her soft hours,
Let's not confound the time with conference harsh.**

Antony to Cleopatra
ANTONY AND CLEOPATRA
Act I, Scene i, Line 44

Please, for the pleasure of Love, let us not destroy this time for love with antagonistic words.

Lust

O, she did so course o'er my exteriors with such a greedy intention that the appetite of her eye did seem to scorch me up like a burning-glass!

Falstaff to Pistol and Nym
MERRY WIVES OF WINDSOR
Act I, Scene iii, Line 59

She looked at me with such passion and desire in her eye that she seemed to burn into me as a magnifying glass concentrates the rays of the sun.

How shall I be revenged on him? I think the best way were to entertain him with hope, till the wicked fire of lust have melted him in his own grease.

Mrs. Ford to Mrs. Page
MERRY WIVES OF WINDSOR
Act II, Scene i, Line 59

How shall I get revenge? I think the best way is to lead him on until the heat of lust consumes him.

Mankind

What a piece of work is a man, how noble in reason, how infinite in faculties; in form and moving how express and admirable, in action how like an angel, in apprehension how like a god: the beauty of the world, the paragon of animals!

Hamlet to R & G
HAMLET
Act II, Scene ii, Line 300

What a marvelous creation man is, how noble in reasoning, how many skills he has, his form and movement well-framed and well done, his good deeds like that of an angel, in understanding, how like a god: he is best of the world, the highest of the animals!

Marriage

Thou art an elm, my husband, I a vine, Whose weakness married to thy stronger state Makes me with thy strength to communicate.

Adriana to Antipholus S.
COMEDY OF ERRORS
Act II, Scene ii, Line 173

When a woman marries, she improves her position because of the status of her husband.

Marriage (cont'd)

Men are April when they woo, December when they wed. Maids are May when they are maids, but the sky changes when they are wives.
Rosalind to Orlando
AS YOU LIKE IT
Act IV, Scene i, Line 134

Men and women change from a spring-like attitude during courtship to a winter-like attitude after they are married.

A young man married is a man that's marred.
Parolles to Bertram
ALL'S WELL THAT ENDS WELL
Act II, Scene iii, Line 292

A young man that marries greatly disturbs his well being.

**Marriage is a matter of more worth
Than to be dealt in by attorneyship.**
Suffolk to all
1 HENRY VI
Act V, Scene v, Line 55

Marriage is demeaned if it arranged on the basis of financial considerations.

Marriage (cont'd)

For what is wedlock forcèd but a hell,
An age of discord and continual strife?
Whereas the contrary bringeth bliss
And is a pattern of celestial peace.

Suffolk to all
1 HENRY VI
Act V, Scene v, Line 62

If marriage is forced it is like a living hell, whereas a willing marriage is wonderful.

Should all despair
That hath revolted wives, the tenth of mankind
Would hang themselves.

Leontes to sons
WINTER'S TALE
Act I, Scene ii, Line 197

If all the men who have wives who don't obey them should despair, one tenth of the men would kill themselves.

Marriage (cont'd)

**Thou art worthy to be hanged
That wilt not stay her tongue.**

**Hang all the husbands
That cannot do that feat, you'll leave yourself
Hardly one subject.**

Leontes to Antigonus and response
WINTER'S TALE
Act II, Scene iii, Line 108

You should be hanged if you can't stop your wife from speaking.

If you hung all husbands who cannot accomplish that, there will be very few citizens left.

Medicine

**Canst thou not minister to a mind diseased,
Pluck from the memory a rooted sorrow,
Raze out the written troubles of the brain,
And with some sweet oblivious antidote
Cleanse the stuffed bosom of that perilous stuff
Which weighs upon the heart?**

Macbeth to Doctor
MACBETH
Act V, Scene iii, Line 40

Can't you treat a mentally ill person by removing from the memory some old sorrow and other troubles with some medicine that will clean the stuffed-up bosom which disturbs the innermost thoughts?

Melancholy

**Sweet recreation barred, what doth ensue
But moody and dull melancholy.**
>Abbess to Adriana
>*COMEDY OF ERRORS*
>*Act V, Scene i, Line 78*

If recreation is denied to a person he or she becomes melancholy.

Men

**However we do praise ourselves,
Our fancies are more giddy and unfirm,
More longing, wavering, sooner lost and won,
Than women's are.**
>*Duke to Viola*
>*TWELFTH NIGHT*
>*Act II, Scene iv, Line 31*

We men, in spite of our self-praise, are less steadfast in love than women are.

**We men may say more, swear more, but indeed
Our shows are more than will; for still we prove
Much in our vows, but little in our love.**
>*Viola to Duke*
>*TWELFTH NIGHT*
>*Act II, Scene iv, Line 115*

We men profess our love more than agrees with our true passion; we always prove to be more bombastic than faithful.

Men (cont'd)

**'Tis not a year or two shows us a man.
They are all but stomachs, and we all but food;
They eat us hungerly, and when they are full,
They belch us.**

Emelia to Desdamona
OTHELLO
Act III, Scene iv, Line 103

Not a year or two goes by that we see an unreasonable man. They are all appetite, but after they have satisfied themselves they discard us.

Mercy

**The quality of mercy is not strained;
It droppeth as a gentle rain from heaven
Upon the place beneath.**

Portia to Shylock
MERCHANT OF VENICE
Act IV, Scene i, Line 182

The virtue of mercy is not constrained. It is like a gift from heaven.

Mercy (cont'd)

**We do pray for mercy,
And that same prayer doth teach us all to render
The deeds of mercy.**

Portia to Shylock
MERCHANT OF VENICE
Act IV, Scene i, Line 198

Since we pray for mercy from others, that prayer should teach us to give mercy as well.

**Mercy is not itself that oft looks so;
Pardon is still the nurse of second woe.**

Escalus to Justice
MEASURE FOR MEASURE
Act II, Scene i, Line 267

Mercy is not truly mercy if it is extended too often. To pardon a misdeed always results in a second misdeed.

**Well, believe this:
No ceremony that to great ones 'longs,
Not the king's crown, nor the deputed sword,
The marshal's truncheon, nor the judge's robe,
Become them with one half so good a grace
As mercy does.**

Isabella to Angelo
MEASURE FOR MEASURE
Act II, Scene ii, Line 58

None of the symbols of authority become the holder of them half as much as their being merciful does.

𝔐𝔢𝔯𝔠𝔶 (cont'd)

Sweet mercy is nobility's true badge.
Tamora to Titus
TITUS ANDRONICUS
Act I, Scene i, Line 122

The willingness to be merciful is the true measure of a noble person.

Mercy but murders, pardoning those that kill.
Prince to all
ROMEO AND JULIET
Act III, Scene i, Line 195

If murderers are forgiven and not constrained, this results in them committing more murder.

Nothing emboldens sin so much as mercy.
Senator 1 to Senator 2
TITUS ANDRONICUS
Act III, Scene v, Line 3

Showing mercy to offenders encourages them to commit more offenses.

Merriment

If to be old and merry be a sin, then many an old host that I know is damned.

Falstaff to Prince Hal
1 HENRY IV
Act II, Scene iv, Line 448

If it is a sin to be old and full of fun, then many an old man that I know is going to go to Hell.

Misery

Misery acquaints a man with strange bedfellows.

Trinculo in soliloquy
THE TEMPEST
Act II, Scene ii, Line 38

Being in very difficult circumstances results in an association with people far different than those you normally encounter.

Mistake(s)

**Look what is done cannot be now amended.
Men shall deal unadvisedly sometimes,
Which after-hours gives leisure to repent.**

Richard to Elizabeth
RICHARD III
Act IV, Scene iv, Line 291

Whatever is done cannot now be changed. Men act badly occasionally and later are sorry they did so.

Misunderstanding

**O, pardon me, my lord! It oft falls out,
To have what we would have,
we speak not what we mean.**
Isabella to Angelo
MEASURE FOR MEASURE
Act II, Scene iv, Line 117

When we are intensely arguing in behalf of a viewpoint, we often exaggerate and say things we really don't mean.

Those that understood him smiled at one another and shook their heads; but for mine own part, it was Greek to me.
Casca to Cassius and Brutus
JULIUS CAESAR
Act I, Scene ii, Line 279

Those that understood what he said nodded their heads affirmatively and mutually understood what the speaker had said, even though the speech was given in Greek rather than Latin, which was Greek to me. (This is the origin of the common expression: "I didn't understand; it sounded like Greek to me.")

**But men may construe things after their fashion,
Clean from the purpose of the things themselves.**
Cicero to Casca
JULIUS CAESAR
Act I, Scene iii, Line 34

Men may interpret circumstances from their own perspective, which may well be very different than the truth.

Misunderstanding (cont'd)

**O hateful Error, Melancholy's child,
Why dost thou show to the apt thoughts of men
The things that are not?**

Messala to the heavens
JULIUS CAESAR
Act V, Scene iii, Line 67

Oh, terrible mistake, the consequence of a distraught mind, why do you indicate to the ready mind of man things that are not true?

Modesty

I will chide no breather in this world but myself, against whom I know most faults.

Orlando to Jaques
AS YOU LIKE IT
Act III, Scene ii, Line 267

I will criticize no one other than myself, inasmuch as I know I have many faults–perhaps more than they have.

Money

They say, if money go before, all ways do lie open.

Ford to Falstaff
MERRY WIVES OF WINDSOR
Act II, Scene ii, Line 154

Wealth can buy access.

Moonlight

**How sweet the moonlight sleeps upon this bank!
Here will we sit and let the sounds of music
Creep in our ears; soft stillness and the night
Become the touches of sweet harmony.**

Lorenzo to Jessica
MERCHANT OF VENICE
Act V, Scene i, Line 54

On a beautiful moonlit evening, the sounds of music harmonize well with the quiet stillness of the night.

Mortality

And may not young men die as well as old?

Gremio to Tranio
TAMING OF THE SHREW
Act II, Scene i, Line 393

Is it not possible for young men to die as well as old men? (Another one of the many places where Shakespeare reminds us of the dangers of life.)

**But kings and mightiest potentates must die,
For that's the end of human misery.**

Talbot to Burgundy
1 HENRY VI
Act III, Scene ii, Line 136

The high and the low all share the same end: Death.

Mortality (cont'd)

**Out, out, brief candle!
Life's but a walking shadow, a poor player
That struts and frets his hour upon the stage
And then is heard no more.**

Macbeth to Seyton
MACBETH
Act V, Scene v, Line 23

End, brief life. Life's nothing but an intangible essence that appears on earth for a short time and then is no longer heard from.

**By med'cine life may be prolonged, yet death
Will seize the doctor too.**

Cymbeline to Cornelius
CYMBELINE
Act V, Scene v, Line 29

Although we may extend life for a while by giving a person medicine for his or her illness, death is seen to be inevitable in that even the knowledgeable person who can dispense medicine to extend life will himself or herself die.

**We are such stuff
As dreams are made on, and our little life
Is rounded with a sleep.**

Prospero to Ferdinand
THE TEMPEST
Act IV, Scene i, Line 156

We humans are as ephemeral as dreams, and our short life on earth is preceded by nothing and is followed by nothing.

Music

How sweet the moonlight sleeps upon this bank!
Here will we sit and let the sounds of music
Creep in our ears; soft stillness and the night
Become the touches of sweet harmony.
Lorenzo to Jessica
MERCHANT OF VENICE
Act V, Scene i, Line 54

On a beautiful moonlit evening, the sounds of music harmonize well with the quiet stillness of the night.

The man that hath no music in himself,
Nor is not moved with concord of sweet sounds,
Is fit for treasons, stratagems, and spoils;
The motions of his spirit are dull as night.
Let no such man be trusted.
Lorenzo to Jessica
MERCHANT OF VENICE
Act V, Scene i, Line 83

Any man who cannot make music, nor enjoy music, is likely to perform evil acts and should not be trusted.

If music be the food of love, play on.
Duke to All
TWELFTH NIGHT
Act I, Scene i, Line 1

If music enhances love, continue to play.

Music (cont'd)

He hath songs for man or woman, of all sizes. No milliner can so fit his customers with gloves.

Servant to Clown
WINTER'S TALE
Act IV, Scene iv, Line 190

He is such a good musician that he can play and sing songs for anyone. His songs are so appropriate that they fit the person better than a milliner can fit gloves to the person.

Mystery

Put not yourself into amazement how these things should be; all difficulties are but easy when they are known.

Duke to Provost
MEASURE FOR MEASURE
Act IV, Scene ii, Line 195

Do not get into a state of perplexed confusion about these strange circumstances. Apparent anomalies can be readily explained once the background information is known.

Name

**What's in a name? That which we call a rose
By any other name would smell as sweet.**

Juliet in soliloquy
ROMEO AND JULIET
Act II, Scene ii, Line 43

What's the significance of a name? The flower we call a rose would have the same aroma even if we called it something else.

Nature

**The birds chant melody on every bush,
The snakes lie rollèd in the cheerful sun,
The green leaves quiver with the cooling wind,
And make a checkered shadow on the ground.**

Tamora to Aaron
TITUS ANDRONICUS
Act II, Scene iii, Line 12

The birds sing sweetly everywhere, the snakes bask in the sun, the breeze moves the leaves, resulting in a patchwork shadow on the ground.

Nature (cont'd)

The earth that's nature's mother is her tomb.
What is her burying gave, that is her womb;
And from her womb children of divers kind
We sucking on her natural bosom find;
Many for many virtues excellent,
None but for some, and yet all different.

Friar in soliloquy
ROMEO AND JULIET
Act II, Scene iii, Line 9

The earth, or soil, is a tomb to which all natural life that dies returns, but it is also is the source, a womb, from which all natural life originates. Further, the earth provides the sustenance, it is the bosom, of all the different kinds of life, "children," that are found on earth. All of these children have many excellent uses, "virtues," and there are none that do not have something to contribute, even though they are all different.

For naught so vile that on the earth doth live
But to the earth some special good doth give;
Nor aught so good but, strained from that fair use,
Revolts from true birth, stumbling on abuse.
Virtue itself turns vice, being misapplied,
And vice sometime's by action dignified.

Friar in soliloquy
ROMEO AND JULIET
Act II, Scene iii, Line 17

There is nothing that lives on earth, albeit ugly to human eyes, that doesn't provide some benefit. Further, there's nothing beautiful and apparently very beneficial, which if used inappropriately, will not cause harm. (As an example, poppies immediately come to mind.)

New Beginnings

**Now is the winter of our discontent
Made glorious summer by this sun of York;
And all the clouds that lowered upon our house
In the deep bosom of the ocean buried.**

Richard in Soliloquy
RICHARD III
Act I, Scene i, Line 1

The sun of York is the king, Edward the Fourth, who is a "son" of the York dynasty. Because of this, the quote does not have general application, but is included because it is such a famous quote. Of course, it would have other applicability if another name were substituted for York.

Nobility

True nobility is exempt from fear.

Suffolk to all
2 HENRY VI
Act IV, Scene i, Line 130

Those persons who are truly noble are free of fear.

**That which in mean men we entitle patience
Is pale cold cowardice in noble breasts.**

Duchess to Gaunt
RICHARD II
Act I, Scene ii, Line 33

What we call patience in ordinary men is nothing but cowardice when applied to major public figures.

Nobility (cont'd)

What a piece of work is a man, how noble in reason, how infinite in faculties; in form and moving how express and admirable, in action how like an angel, in apprehension how like a god: the beauty of the world, the paragon of animals!

Hamlet to R & G
HAMLET
Act II, Scene ii, Line 300

What a marvelous creation man is, how noble in reasoning, how many skills he has, his form and movement well-framed and well done, his good deeds like that of an angel, in understanding, how like a god: he is best of the world, the highest of the animals!

**To the noble mind
Rich gifts wax poor when givers prove unkind.**

Ophelia to Hamlet
HAMLET
Act III, Scene i, Line 100

To a noble person, rich gifts lose their value if the giver of the gifts doesn't give them with good and honest intentions.

**Signs of nobleness, like stars, shall shine
On all deservers.**

Duncan to all
MACBETH
Act I, Scene iv, Line 41

Rich rewards will be given to all those that deserve them.

Nobility (cont'd)

**Some kinds of baseness
Are nobly undergone, and most poor matters
Point to rich ends.**

Ferdinand in soliloquy
THE TEMPEST
Act III, Scene i, Line 2

Some lowly work can be performed in a noble manner,
and such pedestrian effort often leads to rich results.

Obsession

**When the mind's free,
The body's delicate. The tempest in my mind
Doth from my senses take all feeling else
Save what beats there.**

Lear to Kent
KING LEAR
Act III, Scene iv, Line 11

When the mind is free of care and anguish, we are quick to sense
bodily discomfort, but when the mind is greatly disturbed, we
lose any feeling aside from that which is in our minds.

Opinion

What's aught but as 'tis valued?
Troilus to Hector
TROILUS AND CRESSIDA
Act II, Scene ii, Line 52

What amounts to anything but on the basis of how people value it?

**What's the matter, you dissentious rogues,
That, rubbing the poor itch of your opinion,
Make yourselves scabs?**
Marcius to crowd
CORIOLANUS
Act I, Scene i, Line 159

What's your complaint, you seditious rogues, that by expressing your inconsequential opinions, you invent miseries?

Opportunity

**There is a tide in the affairs of men
Which, taken at the flood, leads on to fortune;
Omitted, all the voyage of their life
Is bound in shallows and in miseries.**
Brutus to Cassius
JULIUS CAESAR
Act IV, Scene iii, Line 218

There is an opportunity in a man's life which, taken when it presents itself, results in well being. If not taken, the rest of his life is constrained by difficulties.

Opportunity (cont'd)

**Who seeks, and will not take when once 'tis offered,
Shall never find it more.**
Menas, aside
ANTONY AND CLEOPATRA
Act II, Scene vii, Line 82

He who seeks something and then doesn't take it when it is offered, will never find it again.

**I find my zenith doth depend upon
A most auspicious star, whose influence
If now I court not, but omit, my fortunes
Will ever after droop.**
Prospero to Miranda
THE TEMPEST
Act I, Scene ii, Line 181

I find the apex of my fortune depends upon certain fortuitous circumstances which if I now ignore will result in a continuing decline in my well-being.

Optimism

Past and to come seems best; things present, worst.
Archbishop to all
2 HENRY IV
Act I, Scene iii, Line 108

We look at the past with "rose-colored glasses" and we always expect the future to be an improvement, but we're never happy with our present circumstances.

Pain

Where words are scarce, they are seldom spent in vain,
For they breathe truth that breathe their words in
pain.

Gaunt to York
RICHARD II
Act II, Scene i, Line 7

When words are few, they are normally listened to, because those who are in pain speak the truth.

Parting

Good night, good night! Parting is such sweet sorrow
That I shall say good night till it be morrow.

Juliet to Romeo
ROMEO AND JULIET
Act II, Scene ii, Line 185

Parting from you is such a pleasant sorrow that I will continue saying good night until it is no longer night and then I can say good morning.

Passion

**The lives of all your loving complices
Lean on your health; the which, if you give o'er
To stormy passion, must perforce decay.**

Morton to Northumberland
2 HENRY IV
Act I, Scene i, Line 163

The well-being of all your loved ones depends upon your health, which will surely deteriorate if you act in a rage.

**Is not my sorrow deep, having no bottom?
Then be my passions bottomless with them.**

Titus to Marcus
TITUS ANDRONICUS
Act III, Scene i, Line 216

Is not my sorrow so deep that it's bottomless? Therefore, my passions will also be bottomless.

Patience

He that will have a cake out of the wheat must needs tarry the grinding.

Pandarus to Troilus
TROILUS AND CRESSIDA
Act I, Scene i, Line 14

If you have some wheat and you want a cake made from the wheat, you must wait until the wheat is ground. (This, of course, is meant as a simple analogy to apply to any situation where the desired end result requires waiting until some intermediate step(s) is (are) accomplished.)

Patience (cont'd)

**How poor are they that have not patience!
What wound did ever heal but by degrees?**

Iago to Roderigo
OTHELLO
Act II, Scene iii, Line 352

Those who are not patient are at a great disadvantage. After all, a wound can only heal a little by little.

Peace

**A peace is of the nature of a conquest;
For then both parties nobly are subdued,
And neither party loser.**

Archbishop to all
2 HENRY IV
Act IV, Scene ii, Line 89

A negotiated agreement is a kind of conquest because both sides are honorably subdued, but neither side is a loser.

**Sleep dwell upon thine eyes, peace in thy breast!
Would I were sleep and peace, so sweet to rest!**

Romeo to Juliet
ROMEO AND JULIET
Act II, Scene ii, Line 187

I wish you a peaceful restful sleep. Moreover, I wish I were that peace and rest so that I could be with you.

Penitence

**I am sorry that such sorrow I procure,
And so deep sticks it in my penitent heart
That I crave death more willingly than mercy.**

Angelo to Escalus
MEASURE FOR MEASURE
Act V, Scene i, Line 470

I am so sorry that I caused this sorrow, and I feel so bad that I want death more than I want mercy.

Perceptiveness

**He reads much;
He is a great observer, and he looks
Quite through the deeds of men.**

Caesar to Antony
JULIUS CAESAR
Act I, Scene ii, Line 201

He is a keen observer and he looks behind the actions of men to see what their motivations are.

Persistence

**But Hercules himself must yield to odds;
And many strokes, though with a little axe,
Hews down and fells the hardest-timbered oak.**

Messenger to Richard
3 HENRY VI
Act II, Scene i, Line 53

Great strength is subject to protracted attack by large numbers of modest adversaries.

Pettiness

Small things make base men proud.

Suffolk to all
2 HENRY VI
Act IV, Scene i, Line 107

Petty achievements make inferior men proud.

Drones suck not eagles' blood but rob beehives.

Suffolk to all
2 HENRY VI
Act IV, Scene i, Line 110

Ordinary men do not take bold actions, but rather engage in modest endeavors.

Philosophy

I know that the more one sickens the worse at ease he is; and he that wants money, means, and content is without three good friends.

Corin to Touchstone
AS YOU LIKE IT
Act III, Scene ii, Line 22

I know that the sicker one is, the more uncomfortable he is; he that has little money or the means to make it and is not contented is missing three important features in his life.

**I had as lief not be as live to be
In awe of such a thing as I myself.**

Cassius to Brutus
JULIUS CAESAR
Act I, Scene ii, Line 95

I would as soon die as live a life where I would have to worship another human being such as I am.

Philosophy (cont'd)

This is the excellent foppery of the world, that, when we are sick in fortune, often the surfeits of our own behavior, we make guilty of our disasters the sun, the moon, and the stars. An admirable evasion of whore-master man, to lay his goatish disposition on the charge of a star!

Edmund in soliloquy
KING LEAR
Act I, Scene ii, Line 115

This is the foolishness of the world: when we are not doing well, often because of our own excesses, we blame the sun, the moon, and the stars. This is a contrived evasion of lustful man to blame his personal failings on celestial forces.

Nothing can come of nothing.

Lear to Cordelia
KING LEAR
Act I, Scene i, Line 90

If one does not make an effort to achieve a goal, nothing will be accomplished.

Pity

**Those that can pity, here
May, if they think it well, let fall a tear.**

Prologue
HENRY VII
Prologue, Line 5

Those of you who can feel pity, may, if you think it's appropriate, cry a bit.

Plans

**My brain, more busy than the laboring spider,
Weaves tedious snares to trap mine enemies.**
York in soliloquy
2 HENRY VI
Act III, Scene i, Line 339

My brain, busier than a spider making a web, weaves complicated snares to trap my enemies.

Pleasure

No profit grows where is no pleasure ta'en.
Tranio to Lucentio
TAMING OF THE SHREW
Act I, Scene i, Line 39

An activity is not beneficial if the doer does not enjoy the doing.

Pleasure and action make the hours seem short.
Iago to Roderigo
OTHELLO
Act II, Scene iii, Line 361

Pleasurable activities make the time go fast.

Politics

Something is rotten in the state of Denmark.

Marcellus to Horatio
HAMLET
Act I, Scene iv, Line 90

There is something very unsavory going on in this situation.

You praise yourself
By laying defects of judgment to me; but
You patched up your excuses.

Antony to Caesar
ANTONY AND CLEOPATRA
Act II, Scene ii, Line 54

You praise yourself by comparing yourself with defects you assert are mine, but your own defects are merely glossed over.

Possessions

O reason not the need! Our basest beggars
Are in the poorest thing superfluous.
Allow not nature more than nature needs,
Man's life is cheap as beast's.

Lear to Regan and Goneril
KING LEAR
Act II, Scene iv, Line 259

Oh, don't analyze my need! Even our lowest beggars have some excess possessions. Provide no more to a man than what he needs only to survive and he's no better than a beast.

Power

Lions make leopards tame.

Yea, but not change his spots.
>*King Richard to Mobray
>and response
>RICHARD II
>Act I, Scene i, Line 174*

Although power can make people change their actions, it cannot make people change their beliefs.

Praise

**Gentle breath of yours my sails
Must fill, or else my project fails,
Which was to please.**
>*Prospero in Epilogue
>THE TEMPEST
>Epilogue, Line 11*

You must send me off with kind and generous comments, or else I will know that my effort to entertain you has failed.

Prayer

His worst fault is that he is given to prayer; he is something peevish that way; but nobody but has his fault.

Mistress Quickly to Simple
MERRY WIVES OF WINDSOR
Act I, Scene iv, Line 11

His worst fault is that he is always praying; he is rather foolish in that regard, but then, everyone has some fault.

Prediction

**There is a history in all men's lives,
Figuring the nature of the times deceased;
The which observed, a man may prophesy,
With a near aim, of the main chance of things
As yet not come to life, who in their seeds
And weak beginning lie intreasurèd.**

Warwick to King Henry
2 HENRY IV
Act III, Scene i, Line 80

There is a past record in all men's lives revealing the nature of the times gone by, which, when analyzed, makes it possible for a person to predict, with good accuracy, the general probability of events yet to come. These hints are contained in what has come before.

Preparation

Now 'tis the spring, and weeds are shallow-rooted.
Suffer them now, and they'll o'ergrow the garden
And choke the herbs for want of husbandry.
> *Queen to the King*
> *2 HENRY VI*
> *Act III, Scene i, Line 31*

Self-evident with regard to the apparent subject, but this homely wisdom also applies to the running of large political organizations when enemies of the leader are developing.

A little fire is quickly trodden out,
Which, being suffered, rivers cannot quench.
> *Clarence to all*
> *3 HENRY VI*
> *Act IV, Scene viii, Line 7*

A small fire can easily be put out, but if allowed to burn cannot be quenched with a large source of water. (This applies also to the political affairs of men.)

All things are ready, if our minds be so.
> *Henry V to all*
> *HENRY V*
> *Act IV, Scene iii, Line 71*

All our preparations are complete, but only if our resolve is firm as well.

Preparation (cont'd)

> **Stay, my lord,**
> **And let reason with your choler question**
> **What 'tis you go about. To climb steep hills**
> **Requires slow pace at first.**
>
> *Norfolk to Buckingham*
> HENRY VIII
> *Act I, Scene i, Line 129*

Wait and think about what you're going to do before you act in anger. If you want to overcome difficult obstacles, proceed slowly at the beginning.

> **Those that with haste will make a mighty fire**
> **Begin it with weak straws.**
>
> *Cassius to Casca*
> JULIUS CAESAR
> *Act I, Scene iii, Line 107*

Those that would generate in a hurry a major social change use people who are subservient or ideas that seem inconsequential.

Prevention

> **Think him as a serpent's egg**
> **Which hatched would as his kind grow mischievous,**
> **And kill him in the shell.**
>
> *Brutus in soliloquy*
> JULIUS CAESAR
> *Act II, Scene i, Line 32*

Justify political murder on the basis that, although the adversary is powerless now, he will develop despotic powers in the future.

Prey

**O world, how apt the poor are to be proud.
If one should be a prey, how much the better
To fall before the lion than the wolf!**

Olivia to Viola
TWELFTH NIGHT
Act III, Scene i, Line 124

The unfortunate are often proud and would rather succumb to a far superior adversary than a lesser one.

Pride

Pride went before, ambition follows him.

Salisbury to Warwick and York
2 HENRY VI
Act I, Scene i, Line 178

First a man becomes prideful and afterward he wants to make money or improve his position in society.

Prodigality

I can get no remedy against this consumption of the purse. Borrowing only lingers and lingers it out, but the disease is incurable.

Falstaff to Page
2 HENRY IV
Act I, Scene ii, Line 223

I can't figure out how to correct this continual erosion of monetary resources. Borrowing only drags out the condition, but there is no cure.

Profit

No profit grows where is no pleasure ta'en.

Tranio to Lucentio
TAMING OF THE SHREW
Act I, Scene i, Line 39

An activity is not beneficial if the doer does not enjoy the doing.

Ill blows the wind that profits nobody.

Son to dead father
3 HENRY VI
Act II, Scene v, Line 55

It's a very bad development that is not profitable to someone.

Promptness

I will about it; better three hours too soon than a minute too late.
Ford in soliloquy
MERRY WIVES OF WINDSOR
Act II, Scene ii, Line 281

I'll start now. It is better to be three hours too soon than it is to be one minute too late.

Protest

The lady doth protest too much, methinks.
Gertrude to Hamlet
HAMLET
Act III, Scene ii, Line 222

I think the lady protests too much indicating, perhaps, that she is guilty.

Prudence

Since all is well, keep it so.
Wake not a sleeping wolf.
Chief Justice to Falstaff
2 HENRY IV
Act I, Scene ii, Line 145

Do not disturb present well-being by getting involved in potentially troublesome actions.

Prudence (cont'd)

**In cases of defense 'tis best to weigh
The enemy more mighty than he seems.**

Dauphin to all
HENRY V
Act II, Scene iv, Line 43

When planning a defense, it is better to assume the adversary is more formidable than he appears.

**A night is but small breath and little pause
To answer matters of this consequence.**

King to France to Exeter
HENRY V
Act II, Scene iv, Line 145

An overnight delay is very brief to respond to such important matters.

**Things done well
And with a care exempt themselves from fear.**

King to Wosley
HENRY VIII
Act I, Scene ii, Line 88

When things are done carefully and well, the fear of failure is eliminated.

Public Opinion

**Opinion's but a fool, that makes us scan
The outward habit for the inward man.**

King Simonides to a Lord
PERICLES
Act II, Scene ii, Line 56

Public opinion (and in modern terms, the media) is misguided and encourages us to look at superficial characteristics rather than the true character of a man.

Rage

**Thy rage shall burn thee up, and thou shalt turn
To ashes.**

Philip to John
KING JOHN
Act III, Scene ii, Line 344

Your rage shall cause your destruction.

Rashness

Although I joy in thee,
I have no joy of this contract to-night.
It is too rash, too unadvised, too sudden;
Too like the lightning, which doth cease to be
Ere one can say 'It lightens.' Sweet, good night!
This bud of love, by summer's ripening breath,
May prove a beauteous flow'r when next we meet.

Juliet to Romeo
ROMEO AND JULIET
Act II, Scene ii, Line 117

Although I find great pleasure in being with you, I am apprehensive about our pledge tonight. It's too rash, and may be like lightning, which fades before one can say it's there. Good night, and let us see if this beginning of love ripens with time and proves to have beautifully blossomed when we meet again.

My thoughts were like unbridled children, grown
Too headstrong for their mother.

Cressida to Troilus
TROILUS AND CRESSIDA
Act III, Scene ii, Line 115

My thoughts are like undisciplined children, and they are becoming too forceful for me to restrain.

The gods are deaf to hot and peevish vows.

Cassandra to Hector
TROILUS AND CRESSIDA
Act V, Scene iii, Line 16

Fate will not allow ill-considered vows to be achieved.

Reasoning

Sure he that made us with such large discourse,
Looking before and after, gave us not
That capability and godlike reason
To fust in us unused.

Hamlet in soliloquy
HAMLET
Act IV, Scene iv, Line 36

Surely God, who gave us such powerful reasoning power, able to remember the past and consider the future, did not give us these capabilities to lie dormant in us unused.

Blind fear, that seeing reason leads, finds safer
footing than blind reason stumbling without fear.
To fear the worst oft cures the worse.

Cressida to Troilus
TROILUS AND CRESSIDA
Act III, Scene ii, Line 66

It is safer to allow fear to guide reason than to reason coldly without appropriate apprehension. Often fearing the worst prepares one to overcome the worst.

When valor preys on reason,
It eats the sword it fights with.

Enobarbus in soliloquy
ANTONY AND CLEOPATRA
Act III, Scene xiii, Line 199

When valor prevents the use of reason to evaluate a given situation, it causes disadvantage to the valorous.

Rebirth

**Even through the hollow eyes of death
I spy life peering.**

Northumberland to Ross
RICHARD II
Act II, Scene i, Line 270

Even in a deadly situation I see the possibility of improvement or renewal.

Redundancy

**To gild refinèd gold, to paint the lily,
To throw a perfume on the violet,
To smooth the ice, or add another hue
Unto the rainbow, or with taper-light
To seek the beauteous eye of heaven to garnish,
Is wasteful and ridiculous excess.**

Salisbury to John
KING JOHN
Act IV, Scene ii, Line 11

To plate refined gold, ... , or with a torch to try to add to the light of the sun, is wasteful and ridiculous excess.

Redundancy (cont'd)

**When workmen strive to do better than well,
They do confound their skill in covetousness;
And oftentimes excusing of a fault
Doth make the fault the worse by th' excuse.**

Pembroke to John
KING JOHN
Act IV, Scene ii, Line 28

When workmen try to do better than a good job, they destroy what they have done well by trying to do even better and often, by excusing a fault, make the fault look worse than it really is.

Reformation

**They say best men are molded out of faults;
And, for the most, become much more the better
For being a little bad.**

Mariana to Duke
MEASURE FOR MEASURE
Act V, Scene i, Line 436

A man often becomes a superior man if he has the experience of overcoming undesirable characteristics.

Reformation (cont'd)

Presume not that I am the thing I was,
For God doth know, so shall the world perceive,
That I have turned away my former self.
So will I those that kept me company.
Henry V to Falstaff and all
2 HENRY IV
Act V, Scene v, Line 57

Do not assume that I am the same person I was in my youth. For God knows, and people shall soon see, that I am reformed and I will no longer spend time with those I used to.

The breath no sooner left his father's body
But that his wildness, mortified in him,
Seemed to die too.
Canterbury to Ely
HENRY V
Act I, Scene i, Line 25

As soon as his father died, his wild nature appeared to die also.

Regret

Let us not burden our remembrance with
A heaviness that's gone.
Prospero to Alonzo
THE TEMPEST
Act V, Scene i, Line 198

Let us not trouble our memory with an unpleasantness that is no longer with us.

Religion

**In religion,
What damnèd error but some sober brow
Will bless it and approve it with a text,
Hiding the grossness with fair ornament?**

Bassanio to himself and Portia
MERCHANT OF VENICE
Act III, Scene ii, Line 77

When it comes to religion, a clear sin may be rationalized by some serious-looking authority who quotes a passage from the scriptures, thereby obscuring the reality by means of elegant words.

Religious

**When holy and devout religious men
Are at their beads, 'tis much to draw them thence,
So sweet is zealous contemplation.**

Buckingham to Mayor
RICHARD III
Act III, Scene vii, Line 92

When devout men are praying, it is difficult to disturb them.

Remoteness

I do observe you now of late;
I have not from your eyes that gentleness
And show of love as I was wont to have.
You bear too stubborn and too strange a hand
Over your friend that loves you.
Cassius to Brutus
JULIUS CAESAR
Act I, Scene ii, Line 32

I notice that lately you are not as pleasant to me as I have been accustomed to. You are being very cold to me, even though I consider you my very good friend.

Repentance

Look what is done cannot be now amended.
Men shall deal unadvisedly sometimes,
Which after-hours gives leisure to repent.
Richard to Elizabeth
RICHARD III
Act IV, Scene iv, Line 291

Whatever is done cannot now be changed. Men act badly occasionally and later are sorry they did so.

Reproach

Ah, what sharp stings are in her mildest words.
Countess to Steward
ALL'S WELL THAT ENDS WELL
Act III, Scene iv, Line 18

She rebukes in the kindest way.

Reproof

Better a little chiding than a great deal of heartbreak.
Mrs. Page to Mrs. Ford
MERRY WIVES OF WINDSOR
Act V, Scene iii, Line 8

It's better to live with some small complaints than to encounter a heartbreaking difficulty.

Reputation

O, your desert speaks loud; and I should wrong it
To lock it in the wards of covert bosom,
When it deserves, with characters of brass,
A forted residence 'gainst the tooth of time
And razure of oblivion.
Duke to Angelo
MEASURE FOR MEASURE
Act V, Scene i, Line 9

Your merit is outstanding and it would be wrong to suppress knowledge of it. Rather, it deserves being recorded in words cut in brass so that it is given a means to avoid oblivion with the passage of time.

Reputation (cont'd)

**The purest treasure mortal times afford
Is spotless reputation. That away,
Men are but gilded loam or painted clay.**

Mobray to King Richard
RICHARD II
Act I, Scene i, Line 177

The most valuable thing in life is a good reputation. If a man loses that, he is a superficial artifact.

**Men's evil manners live in brass; their virtues
We write in water.**

Griffith to Katherine
HENRY VIII
Act IV, Scene ii, Line 45

Men's vices are remembered; their virtues are forgotten.

**O, he sits high in all the people's hearts;
And that which would appear offense in us,
His countenance, like richest alchemy,
Will change to virtue and to worthiness.**

Casca to Cassius
JULIUS CAESAR
Act I, Scene iii, Line 157

He is very popular and if we commit an apparently offensive deed with his support, it will make the deed appear to be very worthy.

Reputation (cont'd)

The evil that men do lives after them,
The good is oft interrèd with their bones.

Antony to all
JULIUS CAESAR
Act III, Scene ii, Line 75

The bad deeds of men are remembered after they die. The good deeds are often forgotten after they die.

His life was gentle, and the elements
So mixed in him that Nature might stand up
And say to all the world, "This was a man!"

Antony to all
JULIUS CAESAR
Act V, Scene v, Line 73

He had a noble life and the mixture of his characteristics were such that Nature might pronounce, "This was a great man!"

Reputation, reputation, reputation! O, I have lost my reputation! I have lost the immortal part of myself, and what remains is bestial.

Cassio to Iago
OTHELLO
Act II, Scene iii, Line 252

In losing my reputation, I have lost that which would otherwise live after me and I am left as simply an animal.

Reputation (cont'd)

Reputation is an idle and most false imposition; oft got without merit and lost without deserving.

Iago to Cassio
OTHELLO
Act II, Scene iii, Line 258

Reputation is a worthless and untrue designation since it is often gotten without justification and lost unfairly.

**Good name in man and woman
Is the immediate jewel of their souls.
Who steals my purse steals trash; 'tis something, nothing;
'Twas mine, 'tis his, and has been slave to thousands;
But he that filches from me my good name
Robs me of that which not enriches him
And makes me poor indeed.**

Iago to Othello
OTHELLO
Act III, Scene iii, Line 155

A good reputation is the most valuable possession of a man or woman. Mere money is trivial, but when someone robs me of my well-esteemed name he makes me very poor; moreover, the theft doesn't enrich him.

Resourcefulness

**Gnarling sorrow hath less power to bite
The man that mocks at it and sets it light.**
Gaunt to Bolingbroke
RICHARD II
Act I, Scene iii, Line 292

Painful sorrow is not as hurtful to a man if he scorns and defies it.

A good wit will make use of anything. I will turn diseases to commodity.
Falstaff in soliloquy
2 HENRY IV
Act I, Scene ii, Line 234

A clever man can improvise in any situation and turn a disadvantage to a benefit.

**In the reproof of chance
Lies the true proof of men.**
Nestor to Agamemnon
TROILUS AND CRESSIDA
Act I, Scene iii, Line 33

The overcoming of random misfortune is a true demonstration of a man's worth.

Responsibility

**The lives of all your loving complices
Lean on your health; the which, if you give o'er
To stormy passion, must perforce decay.**
Morton to Northumberland
2 HENRY IV
Act I, Scene i, Line 163

The well-being of all your loved ones depends upon your health, which will surely deteriorate if you act in a rage.

Revelation

**Since you know you cannot see yourself
So well as by reflection, I, your glass,
Will modestly discover to yourself
That of yourself which you yet know not of.**
Cassius to Brutus
JULIUS CAESAR
Act I, Scene ii, Line 67

Since it's obvious that you can see yourself best by the observations of others, I will act as a mirror, and without exaggeration I will reveal characteristics you don't know you have.

Revenge

The villainy you teach me I will execute, and it shall go hard but I will better the instruction.
Shylock to Salerio
MERCHANT OF VENICE
Act III, Scene i, Line 62

If you mistreat me I will reciprocate, but even more severely.

How shall I be revenged on him? I think the best way were to entertain him with hope, till the wicked fire of lust have melted him in his own grease.
Mrs. Ford to Mrs. Page
MERRY WIVES OF WINDSOR
Act II, Scene i, Line 59

How shall I get revenge? I think the best way is to lead him on until the heat of lust consumes him.

Righteousness

The peace of heaven is theirs that lift their swords In such a just and charitable war.
Austria to Constance
KING JOHN
Act II, Scene i, Line 35

Warriors have a clear conscience if they are fighting for a worthy cause.

Ripeness

**How many things by season seasoned are
To their right praise and true perfection!**
Portia to Nerissa
MERCHANT OF VENICE
Act V, Scene i, Line 107

How many things are made perfect by coming at the right time.

**Men must endure
Their going hence, even as their coming hither;
Ripeness is all.**
Edgar to Glouster
KING LEAR
Act V, Scene ii, Line 9

Men must endure the process of death even as they endured the process of being born. The readiness to die is the only factor.

Rudeness

Thou art too wild, too rude, and bold of voice.
Bassanio to Gratiano
MERCHANT OF VENICE
Act II, Scene ii, Line 167

You are too undisciplined, too rude, and too outspoken.

Rudeness (cont'd)

This rudeness is a sauce to his good wit,
Which gives men stomach to digest his words
With better appetite.

Cassius to Brutus
JULIUS CAESAR
Act I, Scene ii, Line 297

His caustic manner is an ornament to display his intelligence, which has the effect of getting others to listen to him and enjoy what he is saying.

Rumor

As I travellèd hither through the land,
I find the people strangely fantasied;
Possessed with rumors, full of idle dreams.
Not knowing what they fear, but full of fear.

Bastard to John
KING JOHN
Act IV, Scene ii, Line 143

As I traveled through the land to get here, I found the people full of strange notions. They are distraught with rumors, not knowing what exactly they fear, but nonetheless full of fear.

Rumor (cont'd)

**Rumor is a pipe
Blown by surmises, jealousies, conjectures,
And of so easy and so plain a stop
That the blunt monster with uncounted heads,
The still-discordant wav'ring multitude,
Can play upon it.**

Rumor to Audience
2 HENRY IV
Induction, 15

Rumor is a wind instrument played by surmises, suspicions, and conjectures. The instrument is so easily played upon that the stupid, confused, and always unhappy mass of people can easily make it be heard.

Sadness

Ay me! sad hours seem long.

Romeo to Benvolio
ROMEO AND JULIET
Act I, Scene i, Line 159

Ay me! When one is unhappy, time seem to drag.

Salesmanship

**Let us, like merchants, show our foulest wares
And think perchance they'll sell; if not, the luster
Of the better yet to show shall show the better,
By showing the worst first.**

Ulysses to Nestor
TROILUS AND CRESSIDA
Act I, Scene iii, Line 358

Let us, acting as if we were merchants, present our least acceptable proposals first, hoping to have them agreed to. If not, then our more attractive proposals will appear much better by comparison.

Sarcasm

Look, he's winding up the watch of his wit; by and by it will strike.

Sebastian to all
THE TEMPEST
Act II, Scene i, Line 12

Wait, he's thinking of some clever thing to say; soon he will come out with it.

Satisfaction

He is well paid that is well satisfied.

Portia to Bassanio
MERCHANT OF VENICE
Act IV, Scene i, Line 413

A sense of satisfaction in doing a task is ample compensation.

Self-control

Well, I know not
What counts harsh fortune casts upon my face;
But in my bosom shall she never come
To make my heart her vassal.

Pompey to Caesar
ANTONY AND CLEOPATRA
Act II, Scene vi, Line 53

I don't know what misfortunes I will encounter in the future, but I will never let this woman into my affections and thus become enthralled with her.

Self-deception

Ah, poor our sex! This fault in us I find,
The error of our eye directs our mind.
What error leads must err. O, then conclude
Minds swayed by eyes are full of turpitude.

Cressida to all
TROILUS AND CRESSIDA
Act V, Scene ii, Line 105

Ah, our poor sex. A fault I find in us is the wandering of our eye to attractive men. Then our eye directs our mind which leads to trouble. The conclusion is that minds that are swayed by the eye are depraved. (This line is spoken by a woman in the play, but the evidence is that the fault applies to both sexes.)

Self-deprecation

**Self-love is not so vile a sin
As self-neglecting.**

Dauphin to King of France
HENRY V
Act II, Scene iv, Line 74

Although neither attitude is attractive, it is better to be guilty of self-love than it is to be guilty of self-neglect.

Self-examination

O that you could turn your eyes toward the napes of your necks, and make but an interior survey of your good selves!

Meninius to all
CORIOLANUS
Act II, Scene i, Line 35

Oh that you could make a clear examination of your own character. (Good can be taken in two senses. In the context of the play, good is being used sarcastically.)

Self-harm

Those wounds heal ill that men do give themselves.

Patroclus to Achilles
TROILUS AND CRESSIDA
Act III, Scene iii, Line 229

Self-inflicted harms are not corrected easily.

Self-harm (cont'd)

**To mourn a mischief that is past and gone
Is the next way to draw new mischief on.**
Duke to Brabantio
OTHELLO
Act I, Scene iii, Line 204

To mourn a loss that cannot be retrieved is the surest way to create new problems.

**To willful men
The injuries that they themselves procure
Must be their schoolmasters.**
Regan to Glouster
KING LEAR
Act II, Scene iv, Line 297

The only way to teach willful men is to let them experience the harms that they bring on themselves.

**O that men's ears should be
To counsel deaf, but not to flattery!**
Apemantus in soliloquy
TIMON OF ATHENS
Act I, Scene ii, Line 242

It's unfortunate that men listen to people who flatter them to take advantage of them but not listen to those that tell them the unpleasant truth without regard to other considerations.

Self-interest

> A wretched soul, bruised with adversity,
> We bid be quiet when we hear it cry.
> But were we burd'ned with like weight of pain,
> As much or more we should ourselves complain.
>
> *Adriana to Luciana*
> COMEDY OF ERRORS
> *Act II, Scene i, Line 34*

We are not inclined to listen to the problems of others, but when we encounter similar problems we are quick to complain.

Self-reliance

> Our remedies oft in ourselves do lie,
> Which we ascribe to heaven. The fated sky
> Gives us free scope; only doth backward pull
> Our slow designs when we ourselves are dull.
>
> *Helena in soliloquy*
> ALL'S WELL THAT ENDS WELL
> *Act I, Scene i, Line 208*

Improvement of our circumstances often depends upon our own actions, not Fate. Life gives us free scope; our lack of success is the consequence of our own ineffective efforts. (One might say that Shakespeare is here once again inveighing against horoscopes. Of course, in other places—some of Hamlet's comments for instance—he says just the opposite.)

Self-reliance (cont'd)

**Men at some time are masters of their fates:
The fault is not in our stars,
But in ourselves, that we are underlings.**

Cassius to Brutus
JULIUS CAESAR
Act I, Scene ii, Line 139

At some point men must face the fact that they determine the progress of their lives. It's not decreed by the stars, but rather our failings that result in our being ruled by others.

'Tis in ourselves that we are thus or thus. Our bodies are our gardens, to the which our will are gardeners.

Iago to Roderigo
OTHELLO
Act I, Scene iii, Line 319

We determine what kind of people we are. We are analogous to gardens and our wills are the gardeners.

Come, be a man! Drown thyself? Drown cats and blind puppies!

Iago to Roderigo
OTHELLO
Act I, Scene iii, Line 334

Drowning is appropriate for cats and newborn puppies, but not for men.

Senses

Dark night, that from the eye his function takes,
The ear more quick of apprehension makes.
Wherein it doth impair the seeing sense,
It pays the hearing double recompense.

Hermia in soliloquy
MIDSUMMER NIGHT'S DREAM
Act III, Scene ii, Line 177

When one cannot see because of darkness, the sensitivity of the ear to sound is greatly enhanced.

Sex

Is it not strange that desire should so many years outlive performance?

Poins to Prince Hal
2 HENRY IV
Act II, Scene iv, Line 242

Is it not remarkable that the desire for sex should last many years past the time that a man can actually perform sex?

Ay, so you serve us
Till we serve you; but when you have our roses
You barely leave our thorns to prick ourselves,
And mock us with our bareness.

Diana to Bertram
ALL'S WELL THAT ENDS WELL
Act IV, Scene ii, Line 17

You are very solicitous until you have seduced us, but then you disdain us and mock the loss of our virginity.

Sex (cont'd)

> **I do know,**
> **When the blood burns, how prodigal the soul**
> **Lends the tongue vows.**
>
> *Polonius to Ophelia*
> *HAMLET*
> *Act I, Scene iii, Line 115*

I know very well, when the libido surges, how readily the mind can encourage the voice to speak vows of faithfulness.

> **When the blood is made dull with the act of**
> **sport, there should be, again to inflame it and**
> **to give satiety a fresh appetite, loveliness in favor,**
> **sympathy in years, manners, and beauties.**
>
> *Iago to Roderigo*
> *OTHELLO*
> *Act II, Scene i, Line 224*

After the sex drive subsides from love-making, to revive interest requires a beautiful partner that is similar in age and interests.

Shyness

> **The red wine first must rise**
> **In their fair cheeks; then we shall have 'em**
> **Talk us to silence.**
>
> *Sandys to Wolsey*
> *HENRY VII*
> *Act I, Scene iv, Line 43*

Before women lose their reserve at a party they must first have some wine, the effect of which will be evident by the reddening of their cheeks.

232

Simpleness

**Never anything can be amiss
When simpleness and duty tender it.**
Theseus to all
MIDSUMMER NIGHT'S DREAM
Act V, Scene i, Line 82

When honest conscientious effort is put forth, it is worthwhile—even if it is done by a simple soul.

**How blessèd are we that are not simple men!
Yet nature might have made me as these are;
Therefore I will not disdain.**
Autolycus to Clown
WINTER'S TALE
Act IV, Scene iv, Line 733

How fortunate are those of us who were born with great intelligence. But because we might have been born without such a gift, I will not disdain those that are simple-minded.

Sin

Anything that's mended is but patched; virtue that transgresses is but patched with sin, and sin that amends is but patched with virtue.

Clown to Olivia
TWELFTH NIGHT
Act I, Scene v, Line 42

Something that is repaired is only patched; therefore, a virtuous person that does a wrong only has a bit of sin patched on him or her, and a villainous person that does a good deed has a bit of virtue patched on him or her. (This is a bit of word play spoken by a Clown to entertain his mistress, but it is another instance where Shakespeare points out that there are conflicting subtleties in almost all considerations involving human emotions and actions.)

**Alack, when once our grace we have forgot,
Nothing goes right; we would, and we would not.**

Angelo in soliloquy
MEASURE FOR MEASURE
Act IV, Scene iv, Line 31

When we degrade our finer nature, things go wrong and we get confused and afraid to act.

**I am sorry one so learned and so wise
Should slip so grossly, both in the heat of blood
And lack of tempered judgment afterward.**

Escalus to Angelo
MEASURE FOR MEASURE
Act V, Scene i, Line 466

It grieves me that so well educated and wise a person should err so badly, not only by giving in to sexual desire, but also in reacting improperly later.

Sin (cont'd)

Nothing emboldens sin so much as mercy.
Senator 1 to Senator 2
TITUS ANDRONICUS
Act III, Scene v, Line 3

Showing mercy to offenders encourages them to commit more offenses.

By custom what they did begin
Was with long use accounted no sin.
Gower, as Chorus
PERICLES
Chorus, Line 29

By their (the sinners) becoming accustomed to sinning over a long period, it no longer produced feelings of guilt.

Few love to hear the sins they love to act.
Pericles to Antiochus
PERICLES
Act I, Scene i, Line 93

Few want to hear about their sins, particularly if they greatly enjoy the sinning.

One sin, I know, another doth provoke;
Murder's as near to lust as flame to smoke.
Pericles in soliloquy
PERICLES
Act I, Scene i, Line 138

One kind of sin tends to generate another kind of sin. Murder is as likely to be caused by lust as smoke is to be caused by fire.

Slander

> **No might nor greatness in mortality**
> **Can censure 'scape; back-wounding calumny**
> **The whitest virtue strikes. What king so strong**
> **Can tie the gall up in the slanderous tongue?**
>
> *Duke to Lucio*
> *MEASURE FOR MEASURE*
> *Act III, Scene ii, Line 174*

No great idea or power or virtuous person can avoid the damage that slander can inflict.

> **O place and greatness, millions of false eyes**
> **Are stuck upon thee; volumes of reports**
> **Run with these false, and most contrarious quest**
> **Upon thy doings; thousand escapes of wit**
> **Make thee father of their idle dream,**
> **And rack thee in their fancies.**
>
> *Duke in soliloquy*
> *MEASURE FOR MEASURE*
> *Act IV, Scene i, Line 59*

Persons of great fame or position have millions of people watching them, and many false reports based on devious investigations into their activities are written about without any regard to the facts; they endure great discomfort as a consequence of the fanciful stories.

𝔖𝔩𝔞𝔫𝔡𝔢𝔯 (cont'd)

**Cannot a plain man live and think no harm
But thus his simple truth must be abused
With silken, sly, insinuating Jacks?**
Richard to Grey (and all)
RICHARD III
Act I, Scene iii, Line 51

Isn't it possible that a simple man can mind his own business without being attacked by some slimy, ill-bred men?

**They that stand high have many blasts to shake them,
And if they fall they dash themselves to pieces.**
Margaret to Dorset
RICHARD III
Act I, Scene iii, Line 258

Persons in high political position are constantly attacked and, if they succumb, their careers are destroyed.

Slander (cont'd)

> 'Tis slander,
> Whose edge is sharper than the sword, whose tongue
> Outvenoms all the worms of Nile, whose breath
> Rides on the posting winds and doth belie
> All corners of the world. Kings, queens, and states,
> Maids, matrons, nay, the secrets of the grave,
> This viperous slander enters.
>
> Pisanio to Imogen
> CYMBELINE
> Act III, Scene iv, Line 33

Slander cuts sharper than a sword; it has more venom than all the snakes in the Nile, it spreads faster than the wind, and it tells lies in all the corners of the world about people both high and low. Viperous slander even poisons the secrets of the grave.

Sleep

> O weary night, O long and tedious night,
> Abate thy hours. Shine comforts from the east;
> And sleep, that sometimes shuts up sorrow's eye,
> Steal me a while from mine own company.
>
> Helena in soliloquy
> MIDSUMMER NIGHT'S DREAM
> Act III, Scene ii, Line 431

Oh, let the sunrise come and end this long night and, until then, let sleep give me respite from my worries.

𝔖𝔩𝔢𝔢𝔭 (cont'd)

> **O sleep, O gentle sleep,**
> **Nature's soft nurse, how have I frightened thee,**
> **That thou no more wilt weigh my eyelids down**
> **And steep my senses in forgetfulness?**
>
> *King Henry in soliloquy*
> *2 HENRY IV*
> *Act III, Scene i, Line 5*

Oh, beneficial sleep, what have I done to keep you at bay so that you will no more make my eyes heavy and allow me to slumber in quiet peace?

> **Sleep dwell upon thine eyes, peace in thy breast!**
> **Would I were sleep and peace, so sweet to rest!**
>
> *Romeo to Juliet*
> *ROMEO AND JULIET*
> *Act II, Scene ii, Line 187*

I wish you a peaceful restful sleep. Moreover, I wish I were that peace and rest so that I could be with you.

> **Care keeps his watch in every old man's eye,**
> **And where care lodges sleep will never lie.**
>
> *Friar to Romeo*
> *ROMEO AND JULIET*
> *Act II, Scene iii, Line 35*

Old men worry and that prevents them from sleeping well.

Sleep (cont'd)

Sleep, that knits up the raveled sleeve of care,
The death of each day's life, sore labor's bath,
Balm of hurt minds, great nature's second course,
Chief nourisher in life's feast.

Macbeth to Lady Macbeth
MACBETH
Act II, Scene ii, Line 36

Sleep, that smoothes out the tangled problems of life, that comforts body and mind; coming after a meal, it is the most important nourishment to life.

I wish mine eyes
Would, with themselves, shut up my thoughts.

Alonso to all
THE TEMPEST
Act II, Scene i, Line 184

I wish I could close my eyes and sleep so that I would be able to get my troubles off my mind.

Solace

I have been troubled in my sleep this night,
But dawning day new comfort hath inspired.

Titus to his sons
TITUS ANDRONICUS
Act II, Scene ii, Line 9

I had unpleasant dreams last night, but the dawning of the new day has made me feel much better.

Solitude

I and my bosom must debate a while,
And then I would no other company.
> *Henry V to all*
> *HENRY V*
> *Act IV, Scene i, Line 31*

I must work things over in my mind and, therefore, I would rather be alone.

Sorrow

When you depart from me, sorrow abides
and happiness takes his leave.
> *Leonato to Don Pedro*
> *MUCH ADO ABOUT NOTHING*
> *Act I, Scene i, Line 90*

I am happy when you are near and unhappy when you are gone.

Sorrow breaks seasons and reposing hours,
Makes the night morning and the noontide night.
> *Brakenbury in Soliloquy*
> *RICHARD III*
> *Act I, Scene iv, Line 76*

Sorrow makes summer seem like winter and disrupts normal hours for sleeping and waking.

𝔖orrow (cont'd)

**Gnarling sorrow hath less power to bite
The man that mocks at it and sets it light.**

Gaunt to Bolingbroke
RICHARD II
Act I, Scene iii, Line 292

Painful sorrow is not as hurtful to a man if he scorns and defies it.

**Of comfort let no man speak!
Let's talk of graves, of worms, and epitaphs,
Make dust our paper, and with rainy eyes
Write sorrow on the bosom of the earth.**

King Richard to all
RICHARD II
Act III, Scene ii, Line 144

Let no man speak comforting words. Let us talk of graves, of decay of mortal remains, and of words on gravestones. Let our tears falling on the dusty ground give witness to our sorrows.

**Is not my sorrow deep, having no bottom?
Then be my passions bottomless with them.**

Titus to Marcus
TITUS ANDRONICUS
Act III, Scene i, Line 216

Is not my sorrow so deep that it's bottomless? Therefore, my passions will also be bottomless.

Sorrow (cont'd)

**When sorrows come, they come not single spies,
But in battalions.**
> *Claudius to Gertrude*
> *HAMLET*
> *Act IV, Scene v, Line 78*

When sorrowful events occur , they occur not one at a time, but in large numbers at the same time.

**To mourn a mischief that is past and gone
Is the next way to draw new mischief on.**
> *Duke to Brabantio*
> *OTHELLO*
> *Act I, Scene iii, Line 204*

To mourn a loss that cannot be retrieved is the surest way to create new problems.

**Your cause of sorrow
Must not be measured by his worth, for then
it hath no end.**
> *Ross to Siward*
> *MACBETH*
> *Act V, Scene viii, Line 45*

Your sorrow at his death should not be comparable to the worth of his life, because then you would never stop grieving.

Spectacle

**O for a Muse of fire, that would ascend
The brightest heaven of invention,
A kingdom for a stage, princes to act,
And monarchs to behold the swelling scene!**

Prologue
HENRY V
Prologue, Line 1

Oh for a goddess of the stage endowed with a fiery spirit that would achieve a heaven-like imagination and have a whole kingdom for a stage with princes as actors and kings and queens to observe the expansive scene!

Sport

**O, let the hours be short
Till fields and blows and groans applaud our sport!**

Hotspur to all
1 HENRY IV
Act I, Scene iii, Line 298

Oh, let it be soon that the sounds of fierce competition give evidence to our actions.

Success

Nothing can seem foul to those that win.

King to Prince Hal
1 HENRY IV
Act V, Scene i, Line 8

Even unpleasant occurrences are not disturbing if you have won.

𝔖𝔲𝔠𝔠𝔢𝔰𝔰 (cont'd)

**New honors come upon him,
Like our strange garments, cleave not to their mold
But with the aid of use.**

Banquo to Angus and Ross
MACBETH
Act I, Scene iii, Line 144

He will not be comfortable with the new honors he has received until, like new clothes, he has used them for a while.

𝔖𝔲𝔠𝔠𝔢𝔰𝔰𝔦𝔬𝔫

The younger rises when the old doth fall.

Edmund in soliloquy
KING LEAR
Act III, Scene iii, Line 23

Youth inherits the power when the older generation succumbs to the frailties of age.

**The oldest hath borne most; we that are young
Shall never see so much, nor live so long.**

Edgar to all
KING LEAR
Act V, Scene iii, Line 326

The oldest people have been burdened with the most trying experiences. We young people will never experience so much nor live as long.

Suicide

>**Against self-slaughter
There is a prohibition so divine
That cravens my weak hand.**
>
> *Imogen to Pisanio*
> *CYMBELINE*
> *Act III, Scene iv, Line 76*

Because suicide is prohibited by holy order, my weak hand becomes cowardly.

Sunrise

>**Look, the gentle day,
Before the wheels of Phoebus, round about
Dapples the drowsy east with spots of grey.**
>
> *Don Pedro to all*
> *MUCH ADO ABOUT NOTHING*
> *Act V, Scene iii, Line 25*

Look, in the east there are signs of the sunrise.

>**The grey-eyed morn smiles on the frowning night,
Check'ring the eastern clouds with streaks of light.**
>
> *Friar in soliloquy*
> *ROMEO AND JULIET*
> *Act II, Scene iii, Line 1*

The pleasant sunrise dispels the ominous night as can be seen from the light showing in the eastern clouds.

𝔖𝔲𝔫𝔯𝔦𝔰𝔢 (cont'd)

**Look, love, what envious streaks
Do lace the severing clouds in yonder east.
Night's candles are burnt out, and jocund day
Stands tiptoe on the misty mountain tops.**

Romeo to Juliet
ROMEO AND JULIET
Act III, Scene v, Line 7

Look, light intertwines with the clouds in the east. The stars are gone and the happy day is just showing on the misty mountain tops.

**Yon grey lines
That fret the clouds are messengers of day.**

Cinna to Casca
JULIUS CAESAR
Act II, Scene i, Line 103

Those grey lines in the clouds indicate the arrival of day.

**Look, the morn in russet mantle clad
Walks o'er the dew of yon high eastward hill.**

Horatio to Bernardo and Marcellus
HAMLET
Act I, Scene i, Line 166

Look, morning, clothed in red light, is spreading over that high hill in the east.

Superior

Good reasons must of force give place to better.
Brutus to Cassius
JULIUS CAESAR
Act IV, Scene iii, Line 203

Good reasons are required to be replaced by superior reasons.

Tears

He has strangled his language in his tears.
King to all
HENRY VIII
Act V, Scene i, Line 156

He has become so emotional that he cannot speak.

Temptation

'Tis one thing to be tempted,
Another thing to fall.
Angelo to Escalus
MEASURE FOR MEASURE
Act II, Scene i, Line 17

There's a big difference between being tempted and actually succumbing to the desire.

𝔗emptation (cont'd)

**Most dangerous
Is that temptation that doth goad us on
To sin in loving virtue.**

Angelo in soliloquy
MEASURE FOR MEASURE
Act II, Scene ii, Line 181

The most dangerous temptation is the desire to sin as a consequence of being attracted to a virtuous woman.

**How oft the sight of means to do ill deeds
Make deeds ill done!**

John to Hubert
KING JOHN
Act IV, Scene ii, Line 219

How often the availability of the way to do bad things results in their being accomplished. (Not an opinion endorsed by the NRA in regard to the ready availability of guns.)

Terror

**O, I have passed a miserable night,
So full of fearful dreams, of ugly sights,
That, as I am a Christian faithful man,
I would not spend another such a night
Though 'twere to buy a world of happy days-
So full of dismal terror was the time!**

Clarence to Keeper
RICHARD III
Act I, Scene iv, Line 2

Oh, I have had such a terrible night of nightmares that I swear I would not agree to spend another night like it even if to do so would mean I could spend a lifetime of happy days.

Theater

**Piece out our imperfections with your thoughts:
Think, when we talk of horses, that you see them
Printing their proud hoofs i' th' receiving earth;
For 'tis your thoughts that now must deck our kings,
Carry them here and there, jumping o'er times,
Turning th' accomplishment of many years
Into an hour-glass.**

Prologue
HENRY V
Prologue, Line 23

Use your imagination to fill in the gaps in the play. Imagine that when the actors speak of horses that you can see them pounding the earth with their hoofs. For you must use your mind's eye to dress our kings in fine array, move them from one location to another, and compress historical events that took years to accomplish into a short time on the stage.

Theft

The fox barks not when he would steal the lamb.
Suffolk to the King
2 HENRY VI
Act III, Scene i, Line 55

The fox (a political enemy) barks not (doesn't make his intentions apparent) when he would steal the lamb (when he intends to do some nasty deed).

Thinking

Think upon what hath chanced, and at more time, The interim having weighed it, let us speak Our free hearts each to other.
Macbeth to Banquo
MACBETH
Act I, Scene iii, Line 153

Think about what has happened and later, having thought about it, let us discuss it frankly with one another.

Time

O Time, thou must untangle this, not I; It is too hard a knot for me t' untie!
Viola in soliloquy
TWELFTH NIGHT
Act II, Scene ii, Line 39

Only time will resolve these issues; it's too difficult a situation for me to straighten out.

Time (cont'd)

Defer no time; delays have dangerous ends.
>*Reignier to Charles*
>*1 HENRY VI*
>*Act III, Scene ii, Line 33*

Don't delay because delays result in serious dangers.

But thoughts (the slaves of life) and life (time's fool)
And time, that takes survey of all the world,
Must have a stop.
>*Hotspur to Prince Hal*
>*1 HENRY IV*
>*Act V, Scene iv, Line 80*

Thoughts can be generated only by life, and life is limited by time, and time, that commands all, must end.

We are time's subjects, and time bids be gone.
>*Hastings to all*
>*2 HENRY IV*
>*Act I, Scene iii, Line 110*

We are all ruled by time and right now the time requires we leave.

Well, thus we play the fools with the time, and
the spirits of the wise sit in the clouds and mock us.
>*Prince Hal to Poins*
>*2 HENRY IV*
>*Act II, Scene ii, Line 130*

We waste time and the wisdom of the ages mocks our foolishness.

Time (cont'd)

**Let not virtue seek
Remuneration for the thing it was. For beauty, wit,
High birth, vigor of bone, desert in service,
Love, friendship, charity, are subjects all
To envious and calumniating Time.**

Ulyssis to Achilles
TROILUS AND CRESSIDA
Act III, Scene iii, Line 169

It's useless for virtue to seek praise for past accomplishments. This is because worthwhile characteristics or deeds are all slandered or forgotten with the passage of time.

**I have important business,
The tide whereof is now.**

Diomedes to Achilles
TROILUS AND CRESSIDA
Act V, Scene i, Line 81

I have important business which must be taken care of now.

**There are many events in the womb of time,
which will be delivered.**

Iago to Roderigo
OTHELLO
Act I, Scene iii, Line 365

Many things will happen in the fullness of time.

Time (cont'd)

Pleasure and action make the hours seem short.
Iago to Roderigo
OTHELLO
Act II, Scene iii, Line 361

Pleasurable activities make the time go fast.

Come what come may,
Time and the hour runs through the roughest day.
Macbeth, aside
MACBETH
Act I, Scene iii, Line 148

No matter how difficult the experiences of a given day, time will continue on and the day will come to an end.

The night is long that never finds the day.
Malcom to Macduff
MACBETH
Act IV, Scene iii, Line 240

Only the night of death never finds the day.

Come, gentlemen, we sit too long on trifles
And waste the time which looks for other revels.
King Simonides to all
PERICLES
Act II, Scene iii, Line 92

Come, gentlemen, we are spending too much time involved in trivialities and waste time that would be better spent on other more entertaining activities.

Tragedy

**And worse I may be yet. The worst is not
So long as we can say "This is the worst."**
> *Edgar (aside)*
> *KING LEAR*
> *Act IV, Scene i, Line 27*

We cannot say this is the worst until we can look back and
see an improvement from where we were. Otherwise, things
may perhaps get even worse.

Trap

**The play's the thing
Wherein I'll catch the conscience of the king.**
> *Hamlet in soliloquy*
> *HAMLET*
> *Act II, Scene ii, Line 590*

I'll use the action in the play to prick the conscience of the King
and thereby trap him.

Treason

**Let them not live to taste this land's increase
That would with treason wound this fair land's peace!**
> *Richmond to all*
> *RICHARD III*
> *Act V, Scene v, Line 38*

Do not let those live to benefit from the wealth of the land
who would act in a treasonous manner to break the peace.

Truth

Truth hath better deeds than words to grace it.
Proteus in soliloquy
TWO GENTLEMEN OF VERONA
Act II, Scene ii, Line 18

Deeds serve better than words to adorn truth.

Truth hath a quiet breast.
Mobray to Bolingbroke
RICHARD II
Act I, Scene iii, Line 96

A man who knows he is right is calm and confident.

Where words are scarce, they are seldom spent in vain, For they breathe truth that breathe their words in pain.
Gaunt to York
RICHARD II
Act II, Scene i, Line 7

When words are few they are normally listened to, because those who are in pain speak the truth.

And I can teach thee, coz, to shame the devil— By telling truth. Tell truth and shame the devil.
Hotspur to Glendower
1 HENRY IV
Act III, Scene i, Line 57

I can show you how to thwart the influence of the devil: tell the truth.

Truth (cont'd)

Out with it boldly: truth loves open dealing.
Katherine to Wosley
HENRY VIII
Act III, Scene i, Line 39

Don't hedge around: the truth is most compatible with direct discussion.

Let your mind be coupled with your words.
Diomedes to Cressida
TROILUS AND CRESSIDA
Act V, Scene ii, Line 15

Mean what you say.

The truth you speak doth lack some gentleness.
Gonzalo to Sebastian
THE TEMPEST
Act II, Scene i, Line 133

Your truthful comments are too blunt.

Tyranny

O, it is excellent
To have a giant's strength! But it is tyrannous
To use it like a giant.
Isabella to Angelo
MEASURE FOR MEASURE
Act II, Scene ii, Line 107

It is excellent to have great authority, but it is tyrannous to use it arbitrarily and severely.

Understanding

As you have one eye upon my follies, as you hear them unfolded, turn another into the register of your own, that I may pass with a reproof the easier, sith you yourself know how easy is it to be such an offender.

Ford to Falstaff
MERRY WIVES OF WINDSOR
Act II, Scene ii, Line 169

As you view my follies from your perspective, look also at a compilation of your own, so that you will be less inclined to condemn me since you will be reminded of how easy it is to do foolish things.

**Their understanding
Begins to swell, and the approaching tide
Will shortly fill the reasonable shore,
That now lies foul and muddy.**

Prospero to Ariel
THE TEMPEST
Act V, Scene i, Line 79

Their understanding begins to improve and shortly they will be able to reason clearly, although now their minds are confused.

Unhappiness

You look not well.
You have too much respect upon the world;
They lose it that do buy it with much care.
Gratiano to Antonio
MERCHANT OF VENICE
Act I, Scene i, Line 73

You worry so much about your financial well being that you will do yourself more harm than good.

I hold the world but as the world,
A stage where every man must play a part,
And mine a sad one.
Antonio to Gratiano
MERCHANT OF VENICE
Act I, Scene i, Line 77

I take the world as it comes and I am resigned to a sad life.

Thou seest we are not all alone unhappy:
This wide and universal theater
Presents more woeful pageants than the scene
Wherein we play in.
Duke Senior to all
AS YOU LIKE IT
Act II, Scene vii, Line 135

If you observe those you encounter in the wide world of life, you see many others are living lives more full of woe than your own.

Unhappiness (cont'd)

Why, what's the matter
That you have such a February face,
So full of frost, of storm, and cloudiness?
Don Pedro to Benedict
MUCH ADO ABOUT NOTHING
Act V, Scene iv, Line 40

What's the problem that you appear so disturbed?*

O God, God,
How weary, stale, flat, and unprofitable
Seem to me all the uses of this world!
Hamlet in soliloquy
HAMLET
Act I, Scene ii, Line 132

Oh God, how unpleasant all the activities in life seem to me.

Unkindness

In nature there's no blemish but the mind:
None can be called deformed but the unkind.
Antonio to Viola
TWELFTH NIGHT
Act III, Scene iv, Line 347

Any ugliness in the appearance of a man or woman is trivial compared to the ugliness of the mind when it is unfaithful.

Unsociable

**I am ill, but your being by me
Cannot amend me; society is no comfort
To one not sociable.**

Imogen to Guiderius
CYMBELINE
Act IV, Scene ii, Line 11

I am ill, but you can't make me better since having company is not helpful when one does not want it.

Valor

In a false quarrel there is no true valor.

Benedict to Don Pedro
MUCH ADO ABOUT NOTHING
Act V, Scene i, Line 120

If one does not have a righteous cause, one cannot be truly valorous.

I know him to be valiant.

Marry, he told me so himself; and he said he cared not who knew it.

Orleans to Constable and response
HENRY V
Act III, Scene vii, Line 99

Sarcastic response about a braggart who the first speaker asserts to be valiant.

Valor (cont'd)

**Cowards die many times before their deaths;
The valiant never taste of death but once.**

Caesar to Calphurnia
JULIUS CAESAR
Act II, Scene ii, Line 32

Because of their fear of death, cowards have the sensation of death many times, but valiant people only face death when they actually die.

**He's truly valiant that can wisely suffer
The worst that man can breathe.**

Senator 1 to Alcibiades
TIMON OF ATHENS
Act III, Scene v, Line 31

He's a really admirable man who can endure slander with composure.

**When valor preys on reason,
It eats the sword it fights with.**

Enobarbus in soliloquy
ANTONY AND CLEOPATRA
Act III, Scene xiii, Line 199

When valor prevents the use of reason to evaluate a given situation, it causes disadvantage to the valorous.

Vengeance

**Take heed; for He holds vengeance in His hand
To hurl upon their heads that break His law.**
Clarence to Murderers
RICHARD III
Act I, Scene iv, Line 194

Be careful; God deals with vengeance on those who break His law.

**Vengeance is in my heart, death in my hand,
Blood and revenge are hammering in my head.**
Aaron to Tamora
TITUS ANDRONICUS
Act II, Scene iii, Line 38

I want vengeance and I have a weapon at hand and I feel the emotion very strongly.

Verbosity

He draweth out the thread of his verbosity finer than the staple of his argument.
Holofernes to Nathaniel
LOVE'S LABOR'S LOST
Act V, Scene i, Line 16

His words are so elegant that the meaning of what he is saying is secondary.

Verbosity (cont'd)

They have been at a great feast of languages and stolen the scraps.

> Moth (aside) to Costard
> LOVE'S LABOR'S LOST
> Act V, Scene i, Line 35

Derogatory comment about a conversation with foreign phrases thrown in that are trivial.

He hath a heart as sound as a bell; and his tongue is the clapper, for what his heart thinks, his tongue speaks.

> Don Pedro to Claudio
> MUCH ADO ABOUT NOTHING
> Act III, Scene ii, Line 11

He is a fine honorable fellow who is very straightforward and directly says what he thinks.

A gentleman that loves to hear himself talk and will speak more in a minute than he will stand to in a month.

> Romeo to Nurse
> ROMEO AND JULIET
> Act II, Scene iv, Line 139

He is a man who talks a great deal and says more in a minute than he will ever stand behind.

Verbosity (cont'd)

Fie, what a spendthrift is he of his tongue!
Antonio to all
THE TEMPEST
Act II, Scene i, Line 24

Terrible! He talks too much!

Vice

There is no vice so simple but assumes
Some mark of virtue on his outward parts.
Bassanio to himself and Portia
MERCHANT OF VENICE
Act III, Scene ii, Line 81

There is no vice so obvious that it cannot be made to have some appearance of virtue.

Villainy

The villainy you teach me I will execute, and it shall go hard but I will better the instruction.
Shylock to Salerio
MERCHANT OF VENICE
Act III, Scene i, Line 62

If you mistreat me I will reciprocate, but even more severely.

Virginity

Loss of virginity is rational increase; and there was never virgin got till virginity was first lost.

Parolles to Helena
ALL'S WELL THAT ENDS WELL
Act I, Scene i, Line 123

Loss of virginity leads to the normal population increase; to beget a virgin requires the loss of virginity.

Virtue

Anything that's mended is but patched; virtue that transgresses is but patched with sin, and sin that amends is but patched with virtue.

Clown to Olivia
TWELFTH NIGHT
Act I, Scene v, Line 42

Something that is repaired is only patched; therefore, a virtuous person that does a wrong only has a bit of sin patched on him or her, and a villainous person that does a good deed has a bit of virtue patched on him or her. (This is a bit of word play spoken by a Clown to entertain his mistress, but it is another instance where Shakespeare points out that there are conflicting subtleties in almost all considerations involving human emotions and actions.)

Virtue (cont'd)

From lowest place when virtuous things proceed,
The place is dignified by the doer's deed;
Good alone
Is good without a name.

King to Bertram
ALL'S WELL THAT ENDS WELL
Act II, Scene iii, Line 124

When a humble person performs virtuous deeds, his or her status is dignified by the action. A good person is good even though he or she does not have a title.

Heaven doth with us as we with torches do,
Not light them for themselves; for if our virtues
Did not go forth of us, 'twere all alike
As if we had them not.

Duke to Angelo
MEASURE FOR MEASURE
Act I, Scene i, Line 32

We light torches not for their own sake, but to serve to see where we're going. Similarly, heaven (the creator) endows us with virtues so that we may use them in a positive manner; if we do not, it wouldn't matter if we were virtuous or not.

Virtue is bold, and goodness never fearful.

Duke to Isabella
MEASURE FOR MEASURE
Act III, Scene i, Line 205

Virtue and goodness are unafraid. (This characteristic is common, alas, even in those who think themselves virtuous and good, even if many others do not agree with them.)

Virtue (cont'd)

A heart unspotted is not easily daunted.
Gloucester to Suffolk
2 HENRY VI
Act III, Scene i, Line 100

A person who is not guilty is not easily frightened.

What stronger breastplate than a heart untainted?
Thrice is he armed that hath his quarrel just,
And he but naked, though locked up in steel,
Whose conscience with injustice is corrupted.
King to all
2 HENRY VI
Act III, Scene ii, Line 232

A man with a clear conscience and a just cause is well armed. But a man corrupted with injustice is "naked," however well he is physically armed.

I'll leave my son my virtuous deeds behind,
And would my father had left me no more.
For all the rest is held at such a rate
As brings a thousandfold more care to keep
Than in possession any jot of pleasure.
King to Clifford
3 HENRY VI
Act II, Scene ii, Line 49

My legacy to my son is my virtuous deeds; I wish my father had left me more. All the rest of my possessions require much more effort to maintain them than can be justified by the small amout of pleasure that I derive from them.

Virtue (cont'd)

> **Let not virtue seek**
> **Remuneration for the thing it was. For beauty, wit,**
> **High birth, vigor of bone, desert in service,**
> **Love, friendship, charity, are subjects all**
> **To envious and calumniating Time.**
>
> *Ulyssis to Achilles*
> *TROILUS AND CRESSIDA*
> *Act III, Scene iii, Line 169*

It's useless for virtue to seek praise for past accomplishments. This is because worthwhile characteristics or deeds are all slandered or forgotten with the passage of time.

> **The rarer action is**
> **In virtue than in vengeance.**
>
> *Prospero to Ariel*
> *THE TEMPEST*
> *Act V, Scene i, Line 27*

People are more likely to seek vengeance than to forgive.

Vows

> **The gods are deaf to hot and peevish vows.**
>
> *Cassandra to Hector*
> *TROILUS AND CRESSIDA*
> *Act V, Scene iii, Line 16*

Fate will not allow ill-considered vows to be achieved.

Vows (cont'd)

**It is the purpose that makes strong the vow;
But vows to every purpose must not hold.**
Cassandra to Hector
TROILUS AND CRESSIDA
Act V, Scene iii, Line 23

The strength of a vow depends upon the purpose of the vow.
Some purposes are not worthy to make the vow be fulfilled.

Vulnerability

**I am not made of stones,
But penetrable to your kind entreaties,
Albeit against my conscience and my soul.**
Richard to all
RICHARD III
Act III, Scene vii, Line 224

I am not rigid in my hesitation, but rather I am affected by
your kind requests, although I would much rather not do so.

War

Rich men look sad, and ruffians dance and leap–
The one in fear to lose what they enjoy,
The other to enjoy by rage and war.

Welsh Captain to Salisbury
RICHARD II
Act II, Scene iv, Line 12

The rich are unhappy because they fear to lose their possessions, and the poor are happy at the prospect of gain from the chaos of civil war.

O, let the hours be short
Till fields and blows and groans applaud our sport!

Hotspur to all
1 HENRY IV
Act I, Scene iii, Line 298

Oh, let it be soon that the sounds of war give evidence to our actions.

I am afeard there are few die well that die in a battle.

Williams to Henry V
HENRY V
Act IV, Scene i, Line 134

I'm afraid that few men have their affairs in order when they die in a war.

Warning

Come not between the dragon and his wrath.
Lear to Kent
KING LEAR
Act I, Scene i, Line 122

Do not put yourself in a dangerous position.

Weakness

The weakest kind of fruit
Drops earliest to the ground.
Antonio to all
MERCHANT OF VENICE
Act IV, Scene i, Line 115

Weak men meet an early death.

Willfulness

To willful men
The injuries that they themselves procure
Must be their schoolmasters.
Regan to Glouster
KING LEAR
Act II, Scene iv, Line 297

The only way to teach willful men is to let them experience the harms that they bring on themselves.

Wine

**The red wine first must rise
In their fair cheeks; then we shall have 'em
Talk us to silence.**

Sandys to Wolsey
HENRY VII
Act I, Scene iv, Line 43

Before women lose their reserve at a party they must first have some wine, the effect of which will be evident by the reddening of their cheeks.

Wisdom

Home-keeping youth have ever homely wits.

Valentine to Proteus
TWO GENTLEMEN OF VERONA
Act I, Scene i, Line 2

Youths who do not leave home will always be dull-witted.

The more pity that fools may not speak wisely what wise men do foolishly.

Touchstone to Celia
AS YOU LIKE IT
Act I, Scene ii, Line 80

It's a shame that simple observers are not allowed to comment about the foolish things that so-called wise men do.

𝔚𝔦𝔰𝔡𝔬𝔪 (cont'd)

**This fellow is wise enough to play the fool;
And to do that well craves a kind of wit.**

Viola in soliloquy
TWELFTH NIGHT
Act III, Scene i, Line 58

This fellow is smart enough to play at being a fool, and to act the part well requires a certain kind of intelligence.

**Full oft we see
Cold wisdom waiting on superfluous folly.**

Helena in soliloquy
ALL'S WELL THAT ENDS WELL
Act I, Scene i, Line 100

We often see that a wise man, or a sensible idea, is kept subordinate to a foolish man, or a bad concept.

Why, I say nothing.

Marry, you are the wiser man; for many a man's tongue shakes out his master's undoing.

Parolles to Clown and response
ALL'S WELL THAT ENDS WELL
Act II, Scene iv, Line 21

An unintelligent man is wise to be reticent, for often when he speaks he reveals his shortcomings, which then results in his loss.

𝔚𝔦𝔰𝔡𝔬𝔪 (cont'd)

**Wise men ne'er sit and wail their loss
But cheerly seek how to redress their harms.**

Queen Margaret to all
3 HENRY VI
Act V, Scene iv, Line 1

Smart men do not sit and bemoan their loss, but rather positively try to find a way to correct their problems.

**All places that the eye of heaven visits
Are to a wise man ports and happy havens.**

Gaunt to Bolingbroke
RICHARD II
Act I, Scene iii, Line 275

A wise man accommodates himself to any place on earth where the sun shines.

The amity that wisdom knits not, folly may easily untie.

Ulysses to Nestor
TROILUS AND CRESSIDA
Act II, Scene iii, Line 97

An agreement that is not made with careful evaluation may be broken easily by ill-considered action.

Thou shouldst not have been old till thou hadst been wise.

Fool to Lear
KING LEAR
Act I, Scene v, Line 38

You should have become wise before you got old.

Wisdom (cont'd)

To wisdom he's a fool that will not yield.
>*A Lord to Helicanus and all*
>*PERICLES*
>*Act II, Scene iv, Line 54*

A man is a fool if he does not follow wise advice.

Then wisely, good sir, weigh
Our sorrow with our comfort.
>*Gonzalo to Alonso*
>*THE TEMPEST*
>*Act II, Scene i, Line 8*

Be wise enough to compare favorably the positive aspects of our situation with the problems.

Wives

Wives may be merry and yet honest too.
>*Mrs. Page in soliloquy*
>*MERRY WIVES OF WINDSOR*
>*Act IV, Scene ii, Line 90*

Wives can have fun and yet remain faithful.

Women

Kindness in women, not their beauteous looks, Shall win my love.

Hortensio to Tranio
TAMING OF THE SHREW
Act IV, Scene ii, Line 41

From now on I'm going to love women who are kind, and I'm not going to be looking for beauty. (This is one of the few places in Shakespeare's plays where men give beauty a lower rating than other virtues when it comes to women.)

Do you not know I am a woman? When I think, I must speak.

Rosalind to Celia
AS YOU LIKE IT
Act III, Scene ii, Line 237

Since I am a woman I must speak when I think. (In today's world, some may take umbrage at these words, but it should be remembered that a) they were written hundreds of years ago, and b) Shakespeare likes to poke fun at any and all. Remember, for instance, the line in Hamlet where the gravedigger asserts that everyone in Britain is mad.)

Two women placed together makes cold weather. Pray sit between these ladies.

Chamberlain to Sandys
HENRY VIII
Act I, Scene iv, Line 22

Two women sitting together at a party puts a damper on the festivities. Therefore, sir, please sit between them.

Women (cont'd)

**Women will love her that she is a woman
More worth than any man; men that she is
The rarest of all women.**

Servant to Paulina
WINTER'S TALE
Act V, Scene i, Line 110

Women will love her because she is more honorable than any man. Men will admire her because she is remarkably beautiful.

Worry

**Care is no cure, but rather corrosive,
For things that are not to be remedied.**

Pucelle (Joan of Arc) to all
1 HENRY VI
Act III, Scene iii, Line 3

Worry does not fix problems, but rather aggravates them for situations that cannot be corrected.

**My mind is troubled, like a fountain stirred;
And I myself see not the bottom of it.**

Achilles to Thersites
TROILUS AND CRESSIDA
Act III, Scene iii, Line 303

My mind is disturbed, like water that has been stirred, and I can't see things clearly.

Writing

The poet's eye, in a fine frenzy rolling,
Doth glance from heaven to earth, from earth to heaven;
And as imagination bodies forth
The forms of things unknown, the poet's pen
Turns them to shapes, and gives to airy nothing
A local habitation and a name.

Theseus to all
MIDSUMMER NIGHT'S DREAM
Act V, Scene i, Line 12

The writer's imagination enables him to use his "pen" to transform thoughts to "reality" on paper by formulating them into a context with names and places.

Youth

Such wind as scatters young men through the world
To seek their fortunes farther than at home,
Where small experience grows.

Petruchio to Hortensio
TAMING OF THE SHREW
Act I, Scene ii, Line 48

I have left home, as many do, to try to improve my situation, since staying at home would limit my experience.

𝔜𝔬𝔲𝔱𝔥 (cont'd)

What is love? 'Tis not hereafter;
Present mirth hath present laughter;
What's to come is still unsure.
In delay there lies no plenty,
Then come kiss me, sweet and twenty;
Youth's a stuff will not endure.

Clown to Toby and Andrew
TWELFTH NIGHT
Act II, Scene iii, Line 44

Love is a present pleasure and since the future is uncertain, enjoy youth and love before it expires.

Young hot colts, being raged, do rage the more.

York to Gaunt
RICHARD II
Act II, Scene i, Line 70

Young willful men, being enraged, become even more so.

Young men's love then lies
Not truly in their hearts, but in their eyes.

Friar to Romeo
ROMEO AND JULIET
Act II, Scene iii, Line 67

Young men are fickle and become infatuated easily on the basis of appearance.

◊ Glossary of Words and Phrases ◊
(Arranged by page number)

Page	Word/Phrase	Definition
1	all remedy	any form of remedy
1	past grief	no longer grieved over
1	without regard	should be put out of one's mind
2	pressure	impressed or printed character
3	strange	unusual or strong
4	censure	judgment
6	old host	friendly old man
7	hath borne most	have lived through more trying experiences
8	cloy	to displease by providing too much
9	mar	makes things worse
11	amends	corrective actions
11	joy's soul	the essence of happiness
11	would	would prefer
12	O place, O form	status, title, position
12	seeming	appearance
14	strange confession in thine eye	your demeanor reveals your apprehension
15	acting	actual performance of
15	first motion	initial proposal
15	phantasma	hallucination

Glossary of Words and Phrases

Page	Word/Phrase	Definition
15	troubled in my sleep	had unpleasant dreams
16	rack	stretch out, as on a torture rack. Agonize over.
17	blood	passion
19	death's pale flag	white skin due to death
19	ensign	badge or identifier
19	Ethiop	An Ethiopian, often shortened to Ethiop; this was the name Shakespeare normally used for a very dark-skinned person
21	put meekness in thy breast	be humble
22	advantage	circumspection
22	cates	delicacies
22	summer house	pleasant home used only in the summer
24	high feeding	good invigorating food
24	Lichas	servant of Hercules
24	loose	unrestrained
25	spice and salt that season a man	the characteristics that give a man character and make him interesting
25	superflux	excess luxury
25	take physic, pomp	cure yourselves, you vainglorious ones
26	thou shamest	you diminish, distort
27	crosses	thwartings

Glossary of Words and Phrases

Page	Word/Phrase	Definition
27	**digest**	understand
27	**wit**	intelligence
28	**careful**	mindful
28	**stint**	stop
29	**collied**	murky, covered with coal dust
29	**in a spleen**	in a flash (like a flash of temper)
30	**babbling**	confused, without meaning
31	**breed unnatural trouble**	creates strange mental problems
31	**infected minds**	anguished minds
31	**my stay**	my remaining here rather than leaving
32	**my worldly business makes a period**	my life comes to an end
33	**enforced**	forced, uncomfortable
33	**heart unspotted**	an honorable person
34	**babbling**	confused, without meaning
34	**worse provided**	less prepared
35	**is none**	is not a worthy man
35	**sticking-place**	a notch, specifically the notch that holds the string of a crossbow cranked taut for shooting
35	**sway by**	direct myself

Glossary of Words and Phrases

Page	Word/Phrase	Definition
36	**bid that welcome**	accept misfortune (sharp fate) with stoicism
36	**grace it**	dignify it
36	**of infinite tongue**	of many clever words
37	**swelling**	increasing in anger
37	**taste of death**	succumb to death
38	**in great revenue**	in great abundance
39	**worse provided**	less prepared
41	**conceit**	judge
41	**credit**	reputation, or credibility
42	**nature**	natural human life
42	**sense of death**	psychological awareness of death
42	**to what we fear of death**	compared to what we fear that being dead will be like
43	**enlargement**	freedom
44	**eternal Mover**	God
44	**meddling fiend**	probably refers to the Devil, or it could simply mean one's conscience
44	**scribbled form**	a rough sketch
45	**deep harmony**	impressive music
45	**ends marked**	words at death heeded, or noted
45	**shrouds**	the ropes supporting the masts of a sailing ship

Glossary of Words and Phrases

Page	Word/Phrase	Definition
45	tackle	the rigging of a sailing ship
45	tongues	words
47	drugs	poisonous plants
47	envy	ill will
47	my worldly business makes a period	my life comes to an end
48	death's pale flag	white skin due to the loss of blood circulation
48	ensign	badge or identifier
48	nature	mortal life
48	'tis common	the normal way of life
49	rack	an instrument of torture
49	rub	obstacle, or disconcerting concern
49	shuffled off this mortal coil	cast off this human turmoil
49	vex not his ghost	do not impose on his departing spirit
50	as pictures	like pictures because there is no motion
50	studied in his death	had practiced how he would react to impending death
51	brief candle	life
51	dusty death	comes from "dust to dust"
53	made on	made of

Glossary of Words and Phrases

Page	Word/Phrase	Definition
54	**visor**	mask, camouflage
56	**of infinite tongue**	of many clever words
56	**walk**	are engaged in
57	**fresh**	bright
57	**put on**	display, or expose
57	**the luster of the better**	the more attractive appearance of the better wares
57	**think perchance they'll sell**	hope they will sell
58	**compliment extern**	outward appearance
58	**necessity of present life**	current requirements
58	**the native act and figure of my heart**	what I really believe and intend
59	**in deepest consequence**	in the vital sequel
59	**put on**	incite, commit
60	**black and deep desires**	evil intentions
60	**look like the time**	play up to the occasion
60	**serpent**	poisonous snake
60	**to beguile the time**	to make sly use of the occasion
61	**false**	deceptive

Glossary of Words and Phrases

Page	Word/Phrase	Definition
61	**full meridian**	prime, splendor, the point of the highest altitude of a star
62	**hang loose about him**	too much for him to deal with
63	**market of**	compensation for
63	**more deaf than adders**	quotation from Psalms
64	**coldest**	unlikely
64	**hits**	succeeds
64	**most fits**	most appropriate
65	**scribbled form**	a rough sketch
65	**shrouds**	the ropes supporting the masts of a sailing ship
65	**tackle**	the rigging of a sailing ship
66	**joy**	happy
67	**soul of lead**	I am very despondent
68	**speeds best**	is best understood
69	**action**	skill of gesturing
69	**speak right on**	straightforwardly, just as I think
69	**utterance**	good delivery
69	**wit**	skill of invention
69	**words**	fluency
69	**worth**	public stature

Glossary of Words and Phrases

Page	Word/Phrase	Definition
71	**dissentious**	seditious
73	**approve**	confirm
73	**effects**	consequences
73	**large speeches**	expansive words
73	**unmingled**	unalloyed, or unmixed with baser characteristics
75	**conceits**	ideas
75	**invention**	imagination
75	**swelling**	expanding in grandeur
76	**deck**	array with fine clothes
77	**invisible spirit of wine**	the ability to wine to make a person inebriated
78	**ingredient**	the wine in the cup
78	**inordinate**	excessive
78	**put an enemy in their mouths**	to drink wine; i.e., alcohol
79	**buckle fortune on my back**	require me to assume responsibilities
79	**I am not made of stones**	I am not completely rigid in my attitude
81	**means secure us**	our capabilities make us rash
81	**mere defects**	deficiencies
81	**prove our commodities**	prove to be advantageous

Glossary of Words and Phrases

Page	Word/Phrase	Definition
83	**poison to thy stomach**	is foreign to your nature
83	**soul of goodness**	obscure small measure of goodness
84	**proper deformity**	surface beauty hiding inherent ugliness
84	**put on**	incite, commit
86	**beauteous eye of heaven**	the sun
86	**confound their skill in covetousness**	destroy what they have done well by trying to do even better
87	**blood more stirs**	the excitement is greater
88	**coldest**	unlikely
88	**hits**	succeeds
88	**most fits**	most appropriate
88	**sticking-place**	a notch, specifically the notch that holds the string of a crossbow cranked taut for shooting
89	**befalls myself**	happens to me
89	**confounds**	ruins
90	**factious**	politically active
90	**fall**	diminish
92	**it boots not**	it is no use
92	**now is clay**	dies
93	**contradict**	counter, stop

Glossary of Words and Phrases

Page	Word/Phrase	Definition
93	**crosses**	painful experiences
93	**intents**	intentions
94	**pall**	fail
94	**rough-hew**	shape roughly in trial form
94	**still**	always
95	**readiness is all**	readiness is all that matters
95	**wanton**	irresponsibly playful
96	**coming hither**	the process of birth
96	**going hence**	process of dying
96	**peevish**	foolish
96	**ripeness**	the time decreed by the gods for the fruit to fall from the tree
97	**possessed with**	distraught over or obsessed by
97	**strangely fantasied**	full of strange notions
97	**true nobility**	true character as opposed to a titled position
98	**oppresseth**	diminishes
98	**tell thy errand**	explain your message
99	**faint**	causing fainting
99	**strange confession in thine eye**	your demeanor reveals your apprehension
99	**thrills**	rushes

Glossary of Words and Phrases

Page	Word/Phrase	Definition
99	**would not know**	would rather not learn
102	**In great revenue**	in great abundance
102	**register**	list
102	**sith**	since
103	**ill**	inappropriately
104	**ill-favored**	ugly
106	**bound in charity**	required by religious principles
107	**counts**	tallies, as on a scoring stick
109	**receive as certain**	accept as truth
109	**rub**	difficulty
109	**sink**	ruin
110	**of that feather**	that kind of person
113	**naughty**	wicked
113	**soul of goodness**	obscure small measure of goodness
115	**break faith upon commodity**	renege on agreements when money is involved
115	**pie**	personal belongings
116	**careful**	full of care
116	**flow in grief**	immersed in grief
116	**master**	cure
119	**crosses**	thwartings
121	**rob love**	get someone to like me

Glossary of Words and Phrases

Page	Word/Phrase	Definition
122	**swelling**	increasing in anger
123	**accents**	languages
123	**accidents**	events
124	**honesty**	chasteness
125	**dear man**	worthy man
125	**general good**	welfare of the state
125	**indifferently**	impartially
125	**speed me**	make me prosper
126	**coldest**	unlikely
126	**hits**	succeeds
126	**most fits**	most appropriate
126	**no other medicine**	no other means of obtaining relief
128	**unbidden**	not invited
130	**break faith upon commodity**	renege on agreements when money is involved
130	**idleness**	trifling activities
131	**In great revenue**	in great abundance
131	**compact**	fitted, matched
131	**generous**	intelligent
131	**honest**	chaste
132	**nature**	natural human life
133	**brook**	endure or tolerate

Glossary of Words and Phrases

Page	Word/Phrase	Definition
134	**strange**	unusual or strong
134	**tide**	time, propitious moment
136	**appetites**	sexual interest
136	**frail blood**	susceptible passions
136	**keep a corner in the thing I love for other's uses**	allow my wife to engage in some extramarital activities
138	**offense's gilded hand**	the money-laden hand of the offender.
138	**shove by**	thwart
139	**appear**	can be seen plainly
139	**arm it in rags**	armor, or clothe sin, i.e., lawbreakers, with poverty
139	**hurtless**	without doing any damage
139	**plate sin with gold**	wealthy lawbreakers
139	**pygmy's straw**	it is vulnerable to the slightest attack
140	**oblivious antidote**	opiate, medicine of forgetfulness
140	**raze out**	erase
140	**stuffed**	choked up
141	**mock**	to play with, like a cat with a mouse
141	**now is clay**	dies
142	**begot upon itself, born on itself**	self-engendered

Glossary of Words and Phrases

Page	Word/Phrase	Definition
143	**joy's soul**	the essence of happiness
144	**forbear to**	restrain from
145	**blood**	passion
145	**commeddled**	mixed together
145	**parcel**	"part and parcel"
145	**pipe**	wind instrument
145	**quality**	nature
145	**stop**	the on/off openings in the instrument that determine the sound it produces
145	**to suffer all alike**	to decline together
148	**brief candle**	life
149	**made on**	made of
151	**holding no quantity**	dimensionless, or shapeless, unlovely
152	**cockled**	in a shell
152	**pretty**	foolish.
153	**nature**	life
155	**bosom**	inner self
155	**in her bosom**	privately
155	**unclasp my heart**	tell her of my love
157	**still**	always
157	**will**	true passion

Glossary of Words and Phrases

Page	Word/Phrase	Definition
159	**hind**	deer
160	**purged**	satisfied, or requited
161	**pitch**	a falconry term which means height
161	**pricks like thorn**	painful when unrequited
161	**prodigious**	monstrous
161	**sprung from**	offspring of
162	**attending**	paying attention
162	**bounty**	wish or capacity to give love
162	**faithfully**	truthfully
163	**love's heralds**	those who deliver messages between lovers
164	**for**	because of
164	**I had passed**	I had experienced
164	**is as the very center of the earth**	my love is at the core of my being
164	**more performance**	more promises and actions of true love
164	**strong base and building of my love**	the love that is the foundation of my life
166	**beggary**	impoverishment
167	**confound**	destroy, waste
167	**entertain him with hope**	lead him on

Glossary of Words and Phrases

Page	Word/Phrase	Definition
168	**apprehension**	capable of understanding
168	**express**	well-framed
169	**marred**	at a great disadvantage
170	**that hath revolted wives**	wives that do not do as their husbands tell them to
171	**oblivious antidote**	opiate, medicine of forgetfulness
171	**raze out**	erase
171	**stay her tongue**	stop her from talking
171	**subject**	citizen
172	**still**	always
172	**will**	true passion
174	**still**	always
176	**look what**	whatever
176	**old host**	friendly old man
176	**shall deal**	shall do things
177	**after their fashion**	each in his own way
177	**clean from the purpose**	contrary to the true meaning
177	**construe**	interpret
178	**apt**	impressionable
178	**melancholy's child**	melancholy people fear unreal dangers.
180	**brief candle**	life

Glossary of Words and Phrases

Page	Word/Phrase	Definition
180	**made on**	made of
183	**lie rolled**	lie coiled
183	**what's in a name**	what's the significance of a name
185	**mean**	of humble origins
185	**true nobility**	true character as opposed to a titled position
186	**apprehension**	capable of understanding
186	**express**	well-framed
187	**Baseness**	pedestrian or lowly
187	**point to**	lead to
187	**poor matters**	low level activities
188	**bound in**	confined to
188	**dissentious**	seditious
188	**omitted**	the opportunity is not taken
189	**ever after droop**	always decline
189	**omit**	neglect
189	**zenith**	apex of fortune, or greatest opportunity
190	**breathe**	speak
191	**lean on your health**	depend upon your well-being
191	**passions**	passionate outbursts
192	**a peace**	a negotiated agreement

Glossary of Words and Phrases

Page	Word/Phrase	Definition
193	**I procure**	I have caused
194	**base men**	inferior men, with a narrow outlook
195	**as lief not be as**	I would rather not live than
195	**content**	contentment
195	**such a thing as I myself**	a mere mortal
196	**foppery**	foolishness
196	**if they think it well**	if they think it's appropriate
196	**sick in fortune, often the surfeit**	our fortunes grow sickly, poor, because of our own excesses
197	**tedious**	complicated
198	**poorest thing superfluous**	even some excess possessions
198	**reason**	analyze
198	**than nature needs**	requires for mere survival
200	**figuring**	revealing
200	**intreasured**	stored up
200	**main chance**	general probability
200	**peevish**	foolish
201	**if our minds be so**	preparation is insufficient if our resolve is not firm
202	**choler**	anger

298

Glossary of Words and Phrases

Page	Word/Phrase	Definition
204	**consumption**	sickly, or continual erosion of monetary resources
206	**exempt themselves from fear**	avoid failure
206	**small breath**	a short time period
208	**bud of love**	the beginning of love
208	**contract**	pledge to love
208	**unbridled**	undisciplined
209	**discourse**	power of thought
209	**fust**	to grow moldy
210	**beauteous eye of heaven**	the sun
211	**confound their skill in covetousness**	destroy what they have done well by trying to do even better
212	**heaviness**	concern
212	**mortified**	struck dead
212	**remembrance**	memory
216	**alchemy**	the "science" of changing base metals to gold
216	**countenance**	support
217	**gentle**	noble
217	**immortal part**	the soul, the essence of a man

Glossary of Words and Phrases

Page	Word/Phrase	Definition
217	**so mixed in him**	evenly balanced
218	**false imposition**	unreasonable burden
218	**immediate jewel**	nearest the heart, or the most cherished thing
219	**gnarling**	psychologically painful
219	**mocks at it**	scorns
219	**reproof of chance**	overcoming random misfortune
219	**sets it light**	asserts it does not have a significant impact
219	**to bite**	to hurt
219	**true proof of men**	the valid demonstration of their worth
220	**glass**	mirror
220	**lean on your health**	depend upon your well-being
220	**modestly**	without exaggeration
221	**entertain him with hope**	lead him on
222	**coming hither**	the process of birth
222	**going hence**	process of dying
222	**ripeness**	the time decreed by the gods for the fruit to fall from the tree
223	**digest**	understand
223	**possessed with**	distraught over or obsessed by
223	**strangely fantasied**	full of strange notions
223	**wit**	intelligence
224	**blunt**	stupid
224	**jealousies**	suspicions

Glossary of Words and Phrases

Page	Word/Phrase	Definition
224	**multitude**	ordinary citizens
224	**of so easy and so plain a stop**	easily played upon
224	**pipe**	wind instrument
224	**still**	always
224	**wit**	intelligence
225	**the luster of the better**	the more attractive appearance of the better wares
225	**think perchance they'll sell**	hope they will sell
226	**counts**	tallies, as on a scoring stick
226	**error of our eye**	wandering of our eye (to other attractive men—or women, depending upon which sex is the speaker)
226	**poor our sex**	our poor sex
226	**turpitude**	baseness, depravity
227	**heal ill**	heal poorly
228	**mischief**	misfortune
228	**the next way**	the surest way
228	**they themselves procure**	inflict upon themselves
229	**fated sky**	fateful heavens
230	**some**	a particular

Glossary of Words and Phrases

Page	Word/Phrase	Definition
230	'tis in ourselves	we control what we are like
230	to the which	refers to our bodies, metaphorically like gardens
230	underlings	subservient beings
232	favor	appearance
234	heat of blood	sexual desire
234	tempered judgment	careful consideration
235	love to hear	want to be told about
236	escapes of wit	sallies of comment
236	rack thee	twist thee about
237	Jacks	low-bred, worthless men
238	belie	spread lies over
238	posting	speeding
238	states	people of national importance
238	worms	snakes
240	knits up the ravelled sleeve	smoothes out the tangled skein
240	second course	sleep after food
240	troubled	clouded, confused, distraught with swirling thoughts
241	and then	therefore
241	bosom	inner self

Glossary of Words and Phrases

Page	Word/Phrase	Definition
242	**gnarling**	psychologically painful
242	**mocks at it**	scorns
242	**passions**	passionate outbursts
242	**sets it light**	asserts it does not have a significant impact
242	**to bite**	to hurt
243	**battalions**	in great numbers
243	**mischief**	misfortune
243	**single spies**	one at a time
244	**applaud**	give evidence of
244	**invention**	imagination
244	**swelling**	expanding in grandeur
245	**cleave not to their mold**	do not fit well, are not comfortable
245	**hath borne most**	have lived through more trying experiences
245	**strange**	new
246	**cravens**	makes cowardly
246	**Phoebus**	god who drives the chariot of the sun
247	**fret**	ornamentally interlace
247	**russet mantle clad**	showing a reddish glow
247	**walks o'er the dew**	rises over

Glossary of Words and Phrases

Page	Word/Phrase	Definition
248	**of force**	of necessity
248	**to fall**	to actually perform the act which one is tempted to do
250	**deck**	array with fine clothes
251	**our free hearts**	our thoughts freely
251	**the interim having weighed it**	having had time to think about it
252	**ends**	results or consequences
252	**fool**	dupe, plaything
252	**must have a stop**	a man must die
252	**takes survey of**	oversees
252	**time bids be gone**	requires us to leave
253	**envious and calumniating**	evil-minded and slanderous
253	**seek remuneration**	seek credit or praise
253	**tide**	time, propitious moment
254	**hours seem short**	makes the time pass quickly
254	**night is long**	death
255	**taste this land's increase**	benefit from the economy of the nation
256	**breathe**	speak
256	**shame the devil**	thwart the devil's influence
257	**out with it boldly**	speak up in a straightforward manner

Glossary of Words and Phrases

Page	Word/Phrase	Definition
258	**register**	list
258	**sith**	since
260	**uses of this world**	activities of human life
261	**amend me**	make me better
262	**taste of death**	succumb to death
263	**death in my hand**	a lethal weapon readily available
264	**stand to**	stand behind, affirm steadfastly
267	**heaven**	the creator
268	**heart unspotted**	an honorable person
269	**envious and calumniating**	evil-minded and slanderous
269	**peevish**	perverse
269	**seek remuneration**	seek credit or praise
270	**I am not made of stones**	I am not completely rigid in my attitude
271	**applaud**	give evidence of
271	**die well**	die having resolved their earthly concerns
271	**rage**	violence
271	**to enjoy**	in hope to enjoy
272	**they themselves procure**	inflict upon themselves
275	**cheerly**	cheerfully; that is, with a positive attitude

Glossary of Words and Phrases

Page	Word/Phrase	Definition
275	**eye of heaven**	sun
277	**cold weather**	loss of gaiety at a party
278	**corrosive**	aggravating
278	**not to be**	that cannot be
278	**troubled**	clouded, confused, distraught with swirling thoughts

◊ Shakespeare, Genius or Fraud? ◊

Many ostensibly erudite books have been written on the subject of whether or not William Shakespeare, the man who was born and raised in Stratford-upon-Avon and came from relatively modest origins, actually wrote the massive amount of extraordinary literature attributed to him. The basic doubt often revolves on the question of how a small town merchant's son could have become so knowledgeable on the manners and language of the socially elite, as is reflected by the words of the characters in many of his plays.

The basic thrust of the argument given by the scholars that support Shakespeare's authenticity is that Shakespeare was a "quick study," as we say in modern parlance, who read a great deal, and who kept his eyes and ears open when he did spend time with the elite.

It is interesting to me that the nay-sayers, who base their argument on the ignorance of Shakespeare of "Court" matters, ignore the fact that Shakespeare also wrote a fair bit about the activities of the peasants who appear in his works. Given the gulf that these authors presume to exist between the classes, how then would their nobleman author have been able to accurately portray the peasant scenes?

But to support the authenticity of Shakespeare, I would propose an argument that I have not yet seen presented. It is based on an inference drawn from his historically well-established association with a group of men known as "The King's Men," and before that as "The Lord Chamberlain's Men." They were a small number of (less than a dozen) "sharers" who owned, operated, and performed in a theater originally built by Richard Burbage, who was both a carpenter and an actor. This core group of men maintained a successful commercial and artistic operation that endured for some two decades.

During this time, the social and political pressure exerted by the secular and religious power structure of London–which opposed all theater–was formidable. In addition, the recurrent outbreaks of the plague sometimes led to closing of theaters for periods of a year or more. In spite of these difficulties, this group of men achieved significant commercial success by offering the paying public, consisting of both the elite (in the comfortable balconies) and the groundlings (in the standing-room-only ground floor), artistically brilliant performances.

To achieve this success, clearly this core group of men had to possess outstanding talent. Then, as now, theatrical success rested on three basic requirements:

1. Good acting.
2. Good material. (That is, well-written plays.)
3. Good direction.

From the written record, we know that Shakespeare was not a leading actor in the company. He played the ghost of Hamlet's father, not Hamlet. He played Adam, not Orlando, in "As You Like It," and so forth. Acting could not have been his only contribution.

The bulk of the plays we know were outstanding–they are still being presented four hundred years later.

We must assume that the direction was good, but since the written information we have does not describe who directed the plays, just how the complex organizational effort was effected to transform the spoken lines of the characters written on paper to an actual theatrical performance is unknown. A reasonable assumption is that there was a great deal of discussion among the principals, and that more than once—in fact many times—someone in the group said to Shakespeare something like: "Just what did you have in mind when you have Lear (or Hamlet, or Ophelia, or whoever) say '...'." Now, according to the Shakespeare-Did-Not-Write-The-Plays people, Shakespeare, having just finished merely copying the material he had received from the nobleman who had written them, always gave an answer that was logical enough to make his skilled colleagues continue to think (over the years of producing plays) that he had an insight into the nuances of the script commensurate with that which would be possessed by the actual author. If Shakespeare could have achieved that, he would have been an actor without peer, rather than one of the lessor acting lights in the company!

Aha! would say the Shakespeare-Did-Not-Write-The-Plays people, "his colleagues soon figured out that Shakespeare hadn't written them, but it was a conspiracy among them all to make sure the material kept coming." Maybe so, but almost a decade after Shakespeare had died, what would then motivate the last surviving members of the group, Heminge and Condell, to go through the Herculean effort of publishing the material, and to say such approving things about him in the book's introductory material, if they knew he was a fraud? We will never know for sure, of course, but to me, the dedication of Heminge and Condell to the task of preserving their colleague's legacy speaks loudly in support of its authenticity.

Robert W. Wolfe

◊ Index of Plays ◊

The Comedies

The Comedy Of Errors
Pages: 5, 16, 82, 116, 133, 141, 149, 168, 172, 229.

The Taming Of The Shrew
Pages: 14, 20, 26, 29, 41, 74, 80, 107, 108, 121, 124, 150, 179, 197, 204, 277, 279.

The Two Gentlemen Of Verona
Pages: 150, 151, 256, 273

A Midsummer Night's Dream
Pages: 29, 30, 79, 103, 132, 151, 231, 233, 238, 279.

Love's Labor's Lost
Pages: 152, 263, 264.

The Merchant Of Venice
Pages: 10, 24, 55, 82, 85, 104, 113, 121, 144, 149, 152, 153, 173, 174, 179, 181, 213, 221, 222, 259, 265, 272.

As You Like It
Pages: 3, 17, 91, 104, 124, 147, 153, 154, 155, 169, 178, 195, 259, 273, 277.

Much Ado About Nothing
5, 13, 17, 32, 55, 56, 71, 101, 108, 116, 117, 121, 143, 155, 156, 241, 246, 260, 261, 264.

Twelfth Night, Or What You Will
Pages: 12, 17, 80, 82, 89, 113, 129, 136, 156, 157, 158, 172, 181, 203, 234, 251, 260, 266, 274, 280.

The Merry Wives Of Windsor
Pages: 67, 96, 102, 158, 167, 178, 200, 205, 215, 221, 258, 276.

All's Well That Ends Well
Pages: 64, 88, 102, 104, 118, 125, 126, 148, 159, 169, 215, 229, 231, 266, 267, 274.

Measure For Measure
Pages: 10, 12, 13, 31, 42, 74, 114, 126, 129, 133, 137, 146, 148, 174, 177, 182, 193, 211, 215, 234, 236, 248, 249, 257, 267.

The Histories

1 King Henry The Sixth
Pages: 43, 97, 128, 169, 170, 179, 252, 278.

2 King Henry The Sixth
Pages: 8, 33, 38, 39, 43, 44, 53, 97, 133, 144, 160, 185, 194, 197, 201, 203, 251, 268.

3 King Henry The Sixth
92, 120, 194, 201, 204, 268, 275.

The Tragedy Of King Richard The Third
Pages: 2, 11, 18, 21, 30, 34, 67, 68, 77, 79, 135, 137, 138, 176, 185, 213, 214, 237, 241, 250, 255, 263, 270.

The Life And Death Of King John
Pages: 3, 14, 21, 44, 45, 64, 65, 66, 86, 92, 97, 105, 106, 115, 140, 130, 134, 141, 207, 210, 211, 221, 223, 249.

The Tragedy Of King Richard The Second
Pages: 27, 45, 46, 69, 98, 118, 119, 122, 127, 185, 190, 199, 210, 216, 219, 242, 256, 271, 275, 280.

1 King Henry The Fourth
Pages: 22, 28, 80, 87, 123, 176, 244, 252, 256, 271.

2 King Henry The Fourth
Pages: 14, 24, 32, 34, 39, 46, 47, 72, 93, 98, 99, 105, 147, 189, 191, 192, 200, 204, 205, 212, 219, 220, 224, 231, 239, 252.

The Life Of King Henry The Fifth
Pages: 22, 36, 56, 75, 76, 81, 83, 90, 113, 135, 201, 206, 212, 227, 241, 244, 250, 261, 271.

The Life Of King Henry The Eighth
Pages: 23, 56, 61, 83, 106, 109, 119, 135, 202, 206, 216, 248, 257, 277.

The Tragedies

Titus Andronicus
Pages: 15, 28, 37, 47, 119, 122, 175, 183, 191, 235, 240, 242, 263.

Romeo And Juliet
Pages: 6, 18, 19, 23, 26, 40, 48, 66, 67, 87, 93, 99, 120, 122, 127, 160, 161, 162, 163, 183, 184, 190, 192, 208, 224, 239, 246, 247, 264, 280.

Julius Caesar
Pages: 9, 15, 27, 33, 37, 40, 41, 57, 69, 90, 109, 120, 123, 125, 177, 178, 188, 193, 195, 202, 214, 216, 217, 220, 223, 230, 247, 248, 262.

Hamlet Prince Of Denmark
Pages: 2, 4, 15, 48, 49, 63, 66, 83, 93, 94, 95, 111, 124, 138, 140, 145, 168, 186, 108, 205, 109, 232, 243, 247, 255, 260.

The History Of Troilus And Cressida
Pages: 11, 20, 23, 25, 38, 57, 63, 70, 73, 74, 100, 102, 103, 114, 125, 127, 131, 134, 143, 146, 164, 188, 191, 208, 209, 219, 225, 226, 227, 253, 257, 269, 270, 275, 278.

Othello The Moor Of Venice
Pages: 58, 59, 75, 77, 78, 84, 95, 110, 136, 141, 142, 144, 164, 165, 166, 173, 192, 197, 217, 218, 228, 230, 232, 243, 253, 254.

King Lear
Pages: 6, 7, 9, 25, 49, 73, 81, 84, 95, 96, 131, 132, 139, 166, 187, 196, 198, 222, 228, 245, 255, 272, 275.

Macbeth
Pages: 1, 3, 10, 26, 31, 35, 50, 51, 59, 60, 61, 62, 68, 85, 88, 89, 140, 148, 171, 180, 186, 240, 243, 245, 251, 254.

The Life Of Timon Of Athens
Pages: 62, 101, 106, 110, 228, 262.

Antony And Cleopatra
Pages: 7, 8, 36, 91, 100, 103, 107, 112, 130, 145, 166, 167, 189, 198, 209, 226, 262.

Coriolanus
Pages: 71, 72, 188, 227.

The Romances

Pericles Prince Of Tyre
Pages: 53, 54, 70, 126, 128, 207, 235, 254, 276.

Cymbeline
Pages: 52, 72, 107, 112, 139, 180, 238, 246, 261.

The Winter's Tale
Pages: 1, 69, 137, 170, 171, 182, 233, 278.

The Tempest
Pages: 4, 16, 53, 81, 96, 111, 149, 176, 180, 187, 189, 199, 212, 225, 240, 257, 258, 265, 269, 276.

Robert Wolfe was born in Newark, New Jersey, in 1929, and grew up in the nearby town of North Arlington. He graduated from Pratt Institute with a BSME in 1951 and from Drexel Institute with a MSME in 1956. He was employed as an engineer for Westinghouse Electric Corporation for 43 years, and worked at the corporate Science and Technology Center in Pittsburgh from 1960 until his retirement in 1994.

His interest in Shakespeare was heightened by attending The Three Rivers Shakespeare Festival productions in Pittsburgh and by taking several Shakespeare courses at the University of Pittsburgh. In addition to this book, this interest led to the creation of a theatrical presentation in which he appeared as Shakespeare giving a lecture at Oxford in 1615.

Another, less intellectual, interest he pursues is playing tennis and squash, at which he persists in spite of his advancing years and annoying aches and pains. He feels this is a minor penalty to pay for the occasional "thrill of victory" he experiences.